beautiful shrubs
and great climbers

beautiful shrubs
and great climbers
for drama, scent and seasonal interest

richard bird

This edition published by Southwater

This edition distributed in the UK by

The Manning Partnership Ltd
6 The Old Dairy
Melcombe Road
Bath BA2 3LR
tel. 01225 478 444
fax 01225 478 440
sales@manning-partnership.co.uk

This edition distributed in the USA and Canada by

National Book Network
4720 Boston Way
Lanham
MD 20706
tel. 301 459 336
fax 301 459 1705 www.nbnbooks.com

This edition distributed in Australia by

Pan Macmillan Australia
Level 18, St Martins Tower
31 Market St
Sydney, NSW 2000
tel. 1300 135 113
fax 1300 135 103
customer.service@macmillan.com.au

This edition distributed in New Zealand by

The Five Mile Press (NZ) Ltd
PO Box 33–1071 Takapuna
Unit 11/101–111 Diana Drive Glenfield, Auckland 10
tel. (09) 444 4144
fax (09) 444 4518 fivemilenz@clear.net.nz

Southwater is an imprint of Anness Publishing Limited
Hermes House, 88–89 Blackfriars Road, London SE1 8HA
tel. 020 7401 2077; fax 020 7633 9499
www.southwaterbooks.com; info@anness.com

Publisher: Joanna Lorenz
Senior Editor: Caroline Davison
Editors: Deborah Savage, Alison Bolus
Designers: Ian Sandom
Photographers: Johathan Buckley
Production Controller: Joanna King

Previously published in two separate volumes, *Sensational Shrubs* and *Glorious Climbers*

Printed in Hong Kong/China

3 5 7 9 10 8 6 4 2

Half title page: *Salvia officinalis* 'Icterina'
Frontispiece: Honeysuckle.
Title Page: *Rosa* 'Zephirine Drouhin', *Clematis* 'Lady Betty Balfour' and *Vitis coignetiae*.
Above: Pyracantha Hedge.
Opposite (top left): *Choisya ternata*.
Opposite (bottom left): *Rosa* 'Iceberg'.
Opposite (top right): *Campsis radicans*.
Opposite (bottom right): *Rhododendron*.

CONTENTS

INTRODUCTION

Shrubs and climbers are two of the most important groups of plants in any garden. For the casual gardener, they are highly attractive as well as relatively easy to care for, while for the keen gardener, who is perhaps a little more ambitious, they can prove the structural mainstay of the garden design and provide experience in a wide range of useful gardening techniques.

The most successful gardens are those that provide visual interest throughout the year. Although few plants can look stunning all the time, one of the advantages of some shrubs and climbers is that the flowers may be followed by attractive berries in autumn. Many shrubs and climbers are also evergreen, of course, which means that even once the flowers have faded you still have a

Above: *This lilac,* Syringa × henryi, *makes an attractive deciduous shrub with small pink flowers that are very fragrant.*

Above: *Jasmine (*Jasminum*), a climber, can always be relied on to provide a rich, sweet scent in the garden.*

leafy background against which to plant autumn- and winter-flowering bulbs and perennials.

One tends to think of shrubs and climbers in terms of the colour of their flowers – and the contribution these colours can make to your overall planting scheme. However, it is important to remember that the foliage of shrubs and climbers can also bring plenty of colour to the garden, often throughout the year. The colour range includes an infinite variety of greens as well as rich golds, subtle silvers, vivid purples and variegation of all kinds.

In the spring, the flower colours of shrubs and climbers are bright and fresh-looking, including a host of pinks and yellows, while in the autumn they have their final fling with a burst of glorious reds, golds and browns. As well as providing foliage colour and structure all year round, evergreen shrubs – and climbers, too, for that matter – can be invaluable when used as screens or grown as hedges. It should not be forgotten that, as with the flowers, the foliage may be cut and used for indoor decoration, especially in the winter.

Above: *The white flowers of mock orange* (Philadelphus coronarius) *have a wonderfully heady scent, reminiscent of oranges.*

Above: *The Chinese jasmine* (Trachelospermum jasminoides) *is a handsome evergreen climber with very fragrant white flowers.*

Although flower colour is the predominant reason for choosing most plants, the wide variety of shapes and leaf textures is of equal importance. Shrubs, for example, can be round and squat, tall and thin, open like fountains or run flat along the ground. Each of these forms and shapes has its place in the design of the garden. Although it may be the colour of the leaves or the brief flowering period that has the impact, the shape is generally more important. As a silhouette, a tall thin shape seen in the background can be very effective, acting as a focal point and drawing the eye into the distance. This design device can be used to make a garden seem larger than it actually is. Similarly,

a fountain of branches can make a very striking feature. Shrubs with an attractive arching form include the white-flowered *Exochorda* × *macrantha* 'The Bride' and *Spiraea nipponica* 'Snowmound', also with white flowers. Another interesting shape is the evergreen *Mahonia media* 'Charity' which has spikes of scented yellow flowers and large leaves made up of spiny leaflets.

While evergreen shrubs provide effective all-year-round focal points, particularly in the rather less colourful winter months, it is important to remember that other shrubs, too, can have an equally dramatic appearance. For example, the skeletal outline of the branches of many

Above: Euonymus fortunei *'Emerald 'n' Gold' is an evergreen shrub whose variegated leaves have a pink tinge in winter.*

Above: *The flowering climbing* Hydrangea anomala *subsp.* petiolaris *is one of the few climbers that do well in shade, particularly on cool walls.*

deciduous shrubs can look just as beautiful as evergreens against a winter sky or when covered with frost.

Some shrubs can be grown as hedges and used to create barriers, both to keep people and animals from trespassing, and also to provide an element of privacy from the world outside. Hedges have numerous other functions. For example, they make excellent windbreaks, being more effective than a solid boundary, such as a wall, which can create a wind pocket at its base. They also act as a backdrop to the other plants in the border, often contributing much to the overall impact of the colour scheme. Hedges may also create useful screens and dividers within the garden itself, breaking the area down into smaller units. If you are lucky enough to have a large garden, there is nothing more intriguing than wandering from one garden "room" to the next and discovering different designs and colour schemes. In addition, shrubs that are grown as hedges are perfect for screening off ugly utility buildings, such as garages and sheds, or perhaps areas where dustbins (trash cans), oil tanks or washing lines are kept.

Shrubs can also be used to make up the whole of, or just a part of, a border. Unlike herbaceous plants and annuals, they are a constant feature of the border and can be used

Above: *The calico bush (*Kalmia latifolia*) is a magnificent rhododendron-like evergreen with large clusters of cup-shaped flowers.*

Above: *The attractive leaves of the evergreen Oregon grape (*Mahonia aquifolium*) turn wine-red in the winter.*

to provide a permanent planting structure. The various shapes provided by shrubs come into their own here because different shrubs must fit in with and enhance their neighbours in the bed to create a pleasing arrangement. Shrubs can be planted in groups of contrasting varieties, or in a group of one variety for massed effect. Used as a single specimen, they make good focal points, perhaps at the end of a path or in a lawn.

As well as looking good in the border or as specimens in the lawn, shrubs can also be used successfully in containers. They require much more attention than they would get in the open ground, mainly because they need

Above: *The Japanese hydrangea vine (Schizophragma hydrangeoides) is a deciduous climber that attaches to its support by means of aerial roots. The deep green leaves are silvery beneath. The flat flowerheads of creamy flowers are surrounded by lemon-coloured bracts in summer.*

constant watering, but the effort is definitely well worth it, especially if you only have a paved patio or a small balcony in which to garden. Remember that shape is very important when you choose a shrub for planting in a pot because it is usually seen in isolation.

Climbers can also be used as trailing plants and grown down a wall while smaller climbers may hang down from baskets. Why not use climbers, such as clematis, as scrambling plants and allow them to grow over bushes or low trees or simply let them spread across the ground, smothering the weeds as they go? Ivy, with its dense evergreen foliage, is an excellent ground-covering climber. You can also grow climbers up permanent structures such as wooden or metal tripods or use annual varieties in conjunction with temporary structures, such as a wigwam (teepee) of canes or pea-sticks.

Above: *Berberis are mainly grown for their rounded to cup-shaped, usually yellow, flowers. Some varieties are evergreen; the deciduous ones have attractive coloured foliage in autumn.*

Above: *The Etruscan honeysuckle (*Lonicera etrusca*) is a twining, woody-stemmed climber. The pink buds open as fragrant, pale yellow flowers which turn a deeper yellow with age.*

Shrubs and climbers are not difficult to grow. Indeed, in many ways they are amongst the easiest of garden plants to cultivate. The pruning of shrubs and climbers is often considered to be the most difficult aspect of their cultivation but like everything else in gardening it is simply a matter of experience and practice. You cannot be expected to know instinctively how to prune; it is something that must be learnt. Fortunately, it is not difficult and will soon become as easy as slicing bread.

If you are really put off by the thought of pruning, then you can always choose shrubs and climbers that need little or no pruning.

The propagation of shrubs and climbers is not an essential garden task. You can always simply buy your plants from the local garden centre. However, for many people, propagation is one of the most enjoyable aspects of gardening. It is truly magical to take a small seed or piece of stem and turn it into a fully-grown, flourishing plant. Propagation is not difficult; it simply needs a bit of practice.

There are literally thousands of spectacular shrubs and climbers to choose from. In many ways, the choosing is sometimes more daunting than the actual "doing". However, planning and creating a garden is both exciting and rewarding, and whether you thumb through books and catalogues looking for your favourite plants or visit local gardens and nurseries so that you can make a selection from those you see, you will gain a great deal of pleasure when the plants are in your own garden and growing well. After all, pleasure and enjoyment are what gardening is really all about.

Left: *The yew (*Taxus baccata*) is one of the best hedging and topiary plants, its dark green, needle-like leaves forming a dense, impenetrable thicket. It copes well with wind, pollution and drought, and makes a good boundary hedge. The flowers are barely visible, and are followed by small, cup-shaped, red berries. The leaves are highly poisonous. It grows in any good well-drained soil in sun or deep shade. Shown here is one of the Aurea Group.*

Right: Daphne *is a genus of evergreen, semi-evergreen and deciduous shrubs that are largely grown for their tubular flowers. These are usually beautifully scented. This* Daphne × burkwoodii *'Somerset' is a semi-evergreen, upright-growing shrub that produces thick clusters of highly fragrant white and pink flowers in late spring. Occasionally, there is a second burst of flowers in the autumn. Another species,* D. odora, *has fragrant flowers in mid-winter to early spring. Some species of daphne are also grown for their foliage or fruits although the seeds are poisonous.*

GARDENING TECHNIQUES

All the techniques needed to grow shrubs and climbers successfully are simple and often require no more than a little common sense. In this section of the book, as well as explaining how to grow shrubs and climbers, there are detailed instructions on preparing the soil ready for planting, weeding and mulching, and watering and feeding. There is also guidance on specific techniques for shrubs and climbers, including staking shrubs and providing support for climbers. Learning comes with practice, so use this section as a helpful starting point. However, to really know and understand your plants and garden, you will have to go outside and get your hands dirty!

Left: Ampelopsis glandulosa *var.* brevipedunculata *'Elegans' is a vigorous climber grown for its attractive foliage.*

PLANTING AND MAINTENANCE

Soil Preparation

One of the most important of all gardening techniques is soil preparation. It is the foundation of all future growth and success. Since both climbers and shrubs are likely to stay in the same position for many years, it is essential to prepare the ground well before planting. Inadequate attention to preparation at the outset is difficult to remedy once the plant has put down roots and become established.

REMOVING THE WEEDS

The first stage is to rid the ground of weeds. Annual weeds are a minor nuisance and, over a period, they will slowly be eliminated as their seed store in the ground is reduced. The real problem is persistent perennial weeds. If only one piece of these remains, it will soon regrow, and will be impossible to eradicate once the roots become entwined in those of the shrub or climber. In soft, friable soils, these weeds can be removed by hand as the ground is dug over. However, in heavier soils, the only reliable way is to use a chemical weedkiller. Modern herbicides are safe to use as long as the instructions on the packet are rigorously followed.

CONDITIONING THE SOIL

It is important to improve the condition of the soil before you start to plant. Digging is vital, as it breaks up the soil, allowing moisture and air to enter. As you dig the soil, incorporate well-rotted organic material to provide nutrients for the plants' growth. This will also improve drainage in heavy soils, creating a more crumbly consistency, while in light, free-draining soils it will increase retention of water and nutrients.

The best organic material is garden compost, which takes time to prepare: garden waste matter (with woody stems cut into small pieces, or left to rot down first) is piled up together with fruit and vegetable peelings from the kitchen, and left to break down naturally. Well-rotted manure and other proprietary soil conditioners can also be used. If possible, you should prepare an area of at least 1 m (3 ft) in diameter, so that the roots of the shrub or climber can spread out into good soil as they grow.

Above: *Climbers will grow vigorously in good, fertile soil. Here, ivy is being trained around a shape to create topiary.*

Left: *Soil preparation may seem tedious, but it will help to ensure a magnificent display of flowers, as in this* Escallonia *'Gwendolyn Anley'*

MAKING A NEW BED IN A LAWN

1 Choose the site of the bed and mark out its shape. This can be done with a hosepipe (garden hose), moving it around until you have the shape you want. Then dig around it with a spade, lawn edger or hoe.

2 For a circular bed, place a post in the centre of the proposed circle and tie a piece of string to it. Attach a sharp stick or tool at the radius (half the diameter) of the circle and, with the string pulled taut, scribe a circle around the central post. An alternative is to tie a bottle filled with sand to the string and allow the sand to trickle out as you move the bottle round the circle.

3 If the grass contains pernicious and persistent weeds, remove them before digging. The only sure way is to kill them with a herbicide. If the surrounding grass is full of such weeds, these should also be killed or they will soon encroach on the bed.

4 With many lawn grasses, it will not be necessary to use herbicide; simply skim off the surface grass and dig out any roots that remain.

5 Dig the soil, removing any weeds and stones. If possible, double dig the soil, breaking up the lower spit (spade's depth) but not bringing this soil to the surface.

6 Mix plenty of organic material into both layers of the soil, but especially the bottom layer, to encourage the roots to grow deeply.

7 If possible, leave the bed to weather for a few months after digging; then remove any residual weeds that have appeared. When you are ready to plant, add some well-rotted compost or ready-prepared soil conditioner to the soil and lightly fork it in. The weather should have broken the soil down to a certain extent, but the rain will also have compacted it. Lightly fork it over to loosen the soil, break down any lumps and work in any soil conditioner.

8 Rake the soil level, to give it its final tilth, but with a channel round the edge to allow you to trim the edge of the lawn.

Planting Shrubs

There is nothing difficult about planting a shrub, except possibly making the decision as to where to plant it. One thing that must always be borne in mind is that shrubs *do* grow, and it is a common mistake to underestimate by how much. The result is that shrubs are often planted too close together and then the gardener is faced with the heart-rending decision as to which to dig out so that the others can continue to grow. Avoid this by finding out how big the plant will grow and allowing for this when planting. This means there will be gaps between the shrubs for the first few years but these can be temporarily filled with herbaceous perennials and annuals.

PLANTING CARE

If you are planting more than one shrub at a time, stand them all, still in their pots, on the bed in the places where you wish to plant them, so that you can check that they will all fit in and that the arrangement is a good one. Make any adjustments before you begin to plant, as it does the shrubs no good to be dug up and replanted several times because you have put them in the wrong place.

The actual planting is not a difficult process but looking after the plant once it is planted is important. Water it well until it becomes established. If the site is a windy one, protect either the whole bed or individual shrubs with windbreak netting, until they are firmly established. In really hot weather, light shading will help relieve stress on the plant as its new roots struggle to get enough moisture to supply the rapidly transpiring leaves.

Other aspects to consider in positioning shrubs are discussed elsewhere in the book.

PLANTING TIMES

The recommended time for planting shrubs is at any time between autumn and early spring provided that the weather allows you to do so. Planting should not take place if the weather is too wet or too cold or if the ground is waterlogged or frozen.

However this advice is basically for bare-rooted plants – that is, those dug up from nursery beds. Although container-grown plants are easier to establish if planted at the same time, it is possible to plant out at any time of the year as long as the rootball is not disturbed. If planting takes place in the summer, then avoid doing it during very hot or dry weather. The plants will need constant watering and protection from the effects of drying winds and strong sun.

1 Before you start planting, check that the plant has been watered. If not, give it a thorough soaking, preferably at least an hour before planting.

2 If the soil has not been recently prepared, fork it over, removing any weeds. Add a slow-release fertilizer, such as bonemeal, wearing rubber or vinyl gloves if required, and fork this in.

3 Dig the hole, preferably much wider than the rootball of the shrub. Place the plant, still in its pot, in the hole and check that the hole is deep enough by placing a stick or cane across the hole: the top of the pot should align with the top of the soil. Adjust the depth of the hole accordingly.

4 Remove the plant from its pot, being careful not to disturb the rootball. If it is in a plastic bag, cut the bag away rather than trying to pull it off. Place the shrub in the hole and pull the earth back around it. Firm the soil down well around the plant with the heel of your boot and water well.

5 Finally, mulch all around the shrub, covering the soil with 7.5–10 cm (3–4 in) of bark or similar material. This will not only help to preserve the moisture but will also help to prevent weeds from germinating.

Right: *White frothy mounds of flowers are produced by* Spiraea *'Arguta' during the spring. Since it produces its flowers before many other shrubs come into leaf, it can be planted towards the back of the border where it will show up while in flower but then merge into the background for the rest of the year when it is not so striking.*

Planting Climbers

There are so many different types of climbers that you are bound to be able to choose one that is suitable for any place in the garden. As always, though, the trick is to match up the plant and the planting position correctly.

CHOOSING A POSITION

Probably the most important thing to remember about planting a climber is that it is essential to pause and consider whether you are planting it in the right place. Once planted, with the roots spreading and the stems attached to their supports, it is very difficult to move a climber successfully. Once it has grown to its full size, if you realise that you have got the site wrong, you will have a choice of living with your mistake or scrapping the plant and starting all over again with another one. So, think carefully about the position of any climber you plan to introduce.

As well as considering how the climber looks in its intended position, there is a practical consideration. If you are planting against a wall or fence, the plant should be set a distance away, as the ground immediately adjacent to such structures is usually very dry. Similarly, if a pole or post has been concreted in or simply surrounded with rammed earth, it is best for the roots of your climber to be planted a short distance out and the stems led to the support with canes or sticks.

Most plants should be planted at the same depth as they were in their pot or in the nursery bed (usually indicated by the soil line on the stem). The main exception is clematis, which should be planted 5 cm (2 in) deeper, so that the base of the stems is covered.

Mulching around the climber helps to preserve moisture and to keep the weeds down. A variety of methods can be used for mulching; any of them will be of benefit at this stage in helping the climber to establish itself quickly.

PLANTING TIMES

Traditionally, climbers were planted, when the weather allowed, between mid-autumn and mid-spring, but most climbers are now sold as container-grown plants and these can be planted at any time of the year, as long as the weather is not too extreme. Bare-rooted climbers have the best chance of survival if planted at the traditional time. Avoid planting any climber when the weather is very hot and dry, or when there are drying winds. In winter, avoid times when the ground is waterlogged or frozen.

1 Dig over the proposed site for the climber, loosening the soil and removing any weeds that have grown since the ground was prepared. If the ground has not recently been prepared, work some well-rotted organic material into the soil to improve soil texture and fertility.

2 Before planting, add a general or specialist shrub fertilizer to the soil at the dosage recommended on the packet. Work the fertilizer into the soil around the planting area with a fork. A slow-release organic fertilizer, such as bonemeal, is best.

3 Water the plant in the pot. Dig a hole that is much wider than the rootball of the plant. Place the soil evenly around the hole, so that it can easily be worked in around the plant. The hole should be away from any compacted soil, near a support and at least 30 cm (12 in) away from a wall or fence. Before removing the plant from its pot, stand it in the hole, to make certain that the depth and width are correct.

4 Place a cane or stick across the hole; the top of the rootball should be at the same level. Dig deeper or add soil to the bottom of the hole, as necessary, to bring it up to the correct height. Remove the plant from the pot, being careful that none of the soil falls away from the rootball. If the plant is in a polythene (plastic) container rather than a pot, cut the bag away rather than pulling it off. Holding the plant steady, pull in the soil from around the hole, filling in around the rootball. Firm as you go, with your hands, and then finally firm down all around the plant with your foot, making certain that there are no cavities or large air pockets.

5 Train the stems of the climber up individual canes to their main support. Tie the stems in with string or plastic ties. Even twining plants or plants with tendrils will need this initial help. Spread them out, so that they ultimately cover the whole of their support. Water the plant in well.

6 Put a layer of mulch around the plant, to help preserve the moisture and prevent weed growth.

Right: *The delicate bells of* Clematis viticella *hang suspended in mid-air.*

Weeding and Mulching

Keeping your garden weed-free will improve the health and appearance of all your plants. While strong, vigorous plants are able to grow in grass without much difficulty, your shrubs and climbers will benefit from being regularly weeded and protected with a suitable mulch.

WEEDING

Long grass appearing through the lower branches of a bush or growing up through a climber makes the plant look untidy and is difficult to remove. In addition, once the pervasive roots of perennial weeds become entwined among the roots of a plant, they are very difficult to remove. It is therefore essential to prevent weeds from establishing themselves, or at least to remove them as soon as they appear.

Young shrubs in particular do not like competition from weeds. From a health point of view, weeds not only remove vital nutrients and moisture from the soil but, if the shrubs are small, weeds can smother them, preventing light from reaching the foliage. Another disadvantage of allowing weeds to grow under established bushes is that they also provide a constant nuisance by seeding into the surrounding beds and borders.

Prepare the soil thoroughly before planting, so that every piece of perennial weed is either removed by hand or killed off with a herbicide. Once the climber or shrub is planted, weed around it regularly with a hand-fork or hoe, but be careful not to dig too deeply or you may disturb shallow roots lying just below the surface.

USING WEEDKILLER

Unless it is really necessary, it is best to avoid using chemical weedkillers around shrubs. It is so easy to damage or kill the shrub by mistake because most weedkillers will kill or damage whatever they come in contact with. Always follow the instructions on the packet carefully, and keep aside a special watering can to prevent harmful residues killing any of your other plants.

1 Treat deep-rooted weeds like ground elder and bindweed with a translocated weedkiller based on glyphosate, which is moved by the plant to all parts. Use a gel formulation to paint on the weed if watering on the weedkiller is likely to damage plants nearby.

2 If it is possible to water on the weedkiller with a watering can, use a piece of board to shield those plants you don't want to be affected with the weedkiller. If the weeds are not deep-rooted, you could use a contact killer, although it is preferable to use a hoe to remove the weeds if possible.

1 Removing weeds by hand is one of the surest ways of catching them all. Some people find this process tedious but, if carried out regularly, it need not be so. In fact, it is an opportunity to stop and examine the bushes at close quarters, not only to look for problems but to appreciate the plants. Use a small hand-fork but take care not to disturb the roots of established plants.

2 Another method of removing weeds by hand is by hoeing. This is quick and simple, and best carried out in hot weather so that any weeds hoed up quickly die. A large hoe can be used but, for more control in confined areas, a small onion hoe is better.

MULCHING

Mulching has many benefits in the garden: the main one is that it cuts down on the amount of time required for watering and weeding, as it holds the moisture in and makes it difficult for weeds to get through. It will not prevent perennial weeds that are already established from coming up, but it will prevent seed in the soil from germinating. Never mulch over the top of perennial weeds and always ensure that the soil is moist before you mulch, watering the ground if needed. A wide range of mulches can be used. Organic ones are best because they slowly decompose into the soil, adding to its structure and fertility, so benefiting the plant in the longer term as well.

1 Here, the potentilla is surrounded by bare earth. This provides an attractive finish as long as it is weed-free and dug over from time to time, to refresh the surface. But to save on labour in your garden, it is best to add a mulch.

2 Grass clippings make a cheap and effective mulch. Never apply them too thickly – 5 cm (2 in) is the maximum depth – or the heat they produce as they decompose may harm the stems of the plant. Never use mowings from grass that has gone to seed or the mulch could provide the reverse of its intended effect!

3 Chipped or composted bark is a very good mulch. It should be stored for several months to let it release any resin and start to decompose. Some gardeners worry that it introduces fungal diseases, but the spores of these are already in the air and the bark does not appreciably increase the risk.

4 Special black plastic, with holes in it to allow water to pass through to the soil, is readily available from garden centres and nurseries. If you lay the plastic before you plant the climber or shrub, cut holes in it and plant through it. On the other hand, if the plant is already in position, cut the plastic to shape and lay it on the surface of the soil.

5 Plastic would be the perfect mulch were it not so unattractive. However, it can be covered with gravel or small stones. Make certain that the plastic is flat, with no ridges or wrinkles in it that will poke up through the stones, then pour the gravel on to cover the plastic completely.

Above: *Gravel makes an ideal background against which to see the plants. It is easy to maintain and can be raked to keep its fresh appearance. Make certain that the plastic does not show through, as this can spoil the effect.*

Watering

Once shrubs and climbers are established it is not often necessary to water them, unless there are periods of extreme drought. It is, however, important to water them when they are first planted and while they are developing their root system. Lack of attention at this stage can easily kill the plant. Some shrubs show stress much more readily than others. Hydrangeas, for example, are some of the first shrubs whose leaves hang limply when there is a shortage of moisture. They can be used as an indicator that conditions are worsening and that it will soon be time for general watering.

ADVICE ON WATERING

The best water to use on your garden is rain water. If at all possible, it is a very practical idea to use water butts (barrels) or tanks that are connected to the down-water pipe in order to collect any water falling on the roof. However, if you do have to use your tap water, it is important to be careful with hard water that comes from chalky (alkaline) areas. Although your local soil may be acidic, the water from your tap may have been collected miles away, where the soil is alkaline. The golden rule when using tap water is that hard water should not be used on acid-loving or ericaceous plants.

Another useful tip when you are watering your garden with tap water is that it should also be poured first into a barrel and then left to breathe before you use it on your plants. This procedure allows time for any chlorine that has been used in the treatment of the water to be given off.

Selected areas of the garden such as small beds and borders are best watered by hand with a watering can or perhaps a hand-held spray. Larger areas can be dealt with by using a sprinkler. Before you start watering, it is advisable to check to see if there are any local restrictions on the type of watering you may undertake: in drought years or areas of low rainfall, there may well be bans on sprinklers or the use of any method that involves hosepipes (garden hoses).

Whatever method you choose, watering is best carried out in the early morning or evening, when the sun is not too strong. This minimizes wastage of water through evaporation. In addition, drops of water on the plants can act as magnifying lenses, causing the sun to burn small brown spots on the foliage or petals, which though not harmful, are not very attractive. You will also find the chore of watering less arduous on a cool morning rather than in the heat of midday!

1 When watering by hand, have patience and give the ground around the plant a thorough soaking. If in doubt, dig a small hole and check the water has soaked right down to the roots. Sinking tubes around a shrub and pouring water down these is a good way of ensuring the water reaches the right place.

2 A sprinkler has the advantage that you can turn it on and then get on with something else. Place a jam jar or a similar container under the spray, to gauge roughly how much has fallen. There should be at least 2.5 cm (1 in) of water in the jar for the sprinkler to have done any good.

3 A spray attached to a hosepipe (garden hose) can be used as an effective alternative to a sprinkler. This delivers at a greater rate than a sprinkler but, even so, it must still be held in place until the ground is well and truly soaked. It is very easy to under-water using this method, as the gardener can become impatient. Freshen up the plant by spraying over the leaves, to wash away any dirt or dust.

4 A seep (soaker) hose with holes in it is snaked around those plants that need to be watered and left permanently in position. It can be covered with a bark mulch, to hide it. When connected, it provides a slow dribble of water. It is an efficient method of supplying water to exactly where it is needed, avoiding the evaporation that occurs with sprinklers and sprays.

AUTOMATIC WATERING

In areas where there is a constant need to water, a permanent irrigation system employing drip-feed pipes may be well worth considering. Alternatively, you can use a watering system with a timing device, which will save you time and is also beneficial to the plants. There are many systems to choose from, so visit your local garden centre and look at advertisements to find out what is best for your needs.

WATERING ERICACEOUS PLANTS

Ericaceous plants such as rhododendrons and heathers should not be watered with water containing chalk or lime. For this reason, it is advisable not to use tap water on these plants if it is collected from an area with chalky (alkaline) soil. When watering this type of plant, use rain water that has been collected in water butts (barrels) or tanks. Other ericaceous plants include *Andromeda, Camellia, Cassiope, Enkianthus, Gaultheria, Kalmia, Phyllodoce, Pieris* and *Vaccinium.*

1 If you bury a pipeline just beneath the ground you can plug in various watering devices. A sprinkler can be pushed on to this fitting which lies flush with the turf.

2 Control systems can be fitted to the hose system so that you can alter the pressure of the water. These can also act as a filter.

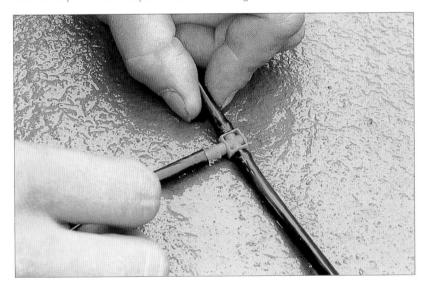

3 Drip-feed systems can be used for beds, borders and containers. "T" joints allow tubes to be attached for individual drip heads.

4 The delivery tube of the hosepipe (garden hose) can be held in position with a pipe peg, if necessary.

Feeding

Most shrubs and climbers do not need regular feeding, particularly if you apply a mulch on a regular basis. Another effective method that cuts down on the amount of feeding you have to do is to allow the leaves to remain on the ground, under and around the plants, so that they will provide a mulch once they have rotted down. When you prepare the soil for planting a new shrub or climber, remember to incorporate plenty of organic material as well as a slow-release fertilizer. This should be sufficient for the plant for at least a year. If more is needed, particularly on light, free-draining soils, a general fertilizer may be applied in spring or a liquid feed in midsummer. The golden rule is never to overfeed.

ADVICE ON FEEDING

As well as water, a plant needs nutrients to keep healthy and produce the maximum number of blooms. These nutrients take the form of minerals and trace elements. In the garden, where plants are more crowded than in nature, the competition for nutrients is intense. If you use an organic mulch regularly, a sprinkling of a slow-release fertilizer, such as bonemeal, may be all that is required for the health of the plant. (When you are handling bonemeal, make sure that you wear vinyl or latex gloves and use a respirator.)

However, when there is regular watering, such as to a plant in a container, the soil can become drained of its nutrients and you will need to replace them. This can be done by adding a dry mixture by hand or by adding a liquid feed. Roses, in particular, benefit from an annual feed, which should be applied in spring or early summer after the dormant season of winter is over.

Whenever possible, choose a slow-release or controlled-release fertilizer that will provide the plant with the nutrients it needs throughout the summer. If you apply fertilizer in the form of concentrated mixes of blood, fish and bone, apply them during warm weather in the spring, when the activity of organisms in the soil will help in their slow release into the soil.

1 Water-soluble fertilizer should be sprinkled around the edges of the shrub, where most of the active root growth is.

2 Gently hoe the fertilizer into the soil in order to help it penetrate the roots more quickly.

3 Water in thoroughly, particularly if the ground is very dry.

OTHER FEEDING METHODS

1 An alternative method of feeding is to use a liquid feed. This is most useful for shrubs or climbers in containers. Add the fertilizer to one of the waterings; in the case of container shrubs, this could be once every three weeks, but it would not be required so frequently in the open soil – once every three months or as recommended by the manufacturer.

2 Granular fertilizer can be applied by hand, spreading it over the area covered by the roots below. Follow the instructions on the bag.

3 Apply a layer of well-rotted organic material, such as farmyard manure or garden compost, to the surface of the soil around the plant. If the plant is not shallow-rooted, lightly fork the material into the top layer of the soil.

Above: *Regular watering and feeding helps to keep plants at their best as the healthy foliage of this* Spiraea japonica *'Goldflame' shows.*

Above: *Walls offer perfect support and protection for climbers. Here,* Rosa *'Zéphirine Drouhin',* Clematis *'Lady Betty Balfour' and* Vitis coignetiae *happily grow together.*

Moving a Shrub

The ideal, when planting shrubs, is to place them in the right position first time round, but, occasionally, it becomes necessary to move one. If the shrub has only been in the ground a few weeks, this is not too much of a problem: simply dig around the plant, lifting it with as big a ball of earth as possible on the spade and move it to a ready-prepared new hole. Moving a well-established shrub requires more thought and planning.

MOVING A WELL-ESTABLISHED SHRUB TO A NEW HOME

If the move is part of a long-term plan, there may well be time to root-prune the shrub first, a few months before you intend to move it. This involves digging a trench or simply slicing a sharp spade into the soil around the shrub, to sever the roots. This encourages the shrub to produce more fibrous feeding roots on the remaining roots and makes it easier for it to become established once it is moved.

Once you have moved the shrub, keep it well-watered and, as with all newly-planted shrubs, if it is in a windy situation, protect it with windbreak netting to prevent excessive transpiration. Shrubs that have been moved are likely to be vulnerable to wind-rock and so it is important to stake them firmly.

A shrub with a large ball of earth around its roots is a very heavy and unwieldy object to move. This can be a recipe for a back injury, so be very careful. Always get somebody to help, if possible. This will also ensure you don't drop the plant, causing the soil around the roots to drop off, which makes it far more difficult to re-establish the plant.

1 If possible, root-prune the shrub a few months before moving, to encourage the formation of new fibrous roots. Water the plant well the day before moving it.

2 Dig a trench around the plant, leaving a rootball that two people can comfortably lift. Sever any roots you encounter to release the rootball.

3 Dig under the shrub, cutting through any tap roots that hold it in place.

4 Rock the plant to one side and insert some hessian (burlap) sacking or strong plastic sheeting as far under the plant as you can. Push several folds of material under the rootball.

5 Rock it in the opposite direction and pull the hessian sacking or plastic sheeting through, so that it is completely under the plant.

6 Pull the sheeting round the rootball so that it completely encloses the soil and tie it firmly around the neck of the plant. The shrub is now ready to move. If it is a small plant, one person may be able to lift it out of the hole and transfer it to its new site.

7 If the plant plus the soil is heavy, it is best moved by two people. This can be made much easier by tying a bar of wood or metal to the trunk of the shrub or to the sacking. With one person on each end, lift the shrub out of the hole.

8 Prepare the ground and hole as for a new shrub and lower the transplanted shrub into it. Follow the reverse procedure, unwrapping and removing the sheeting from the rootball. Ensure the plant is in the right position and refill the hole.

Right: *Once the shrub has been replanted in its new position, water it thoroughly and mulch the soil around it. In more exposed positions place netting round it to prevent winds from drying the plant out and scorching it. It may also need protection from fierce sun. Moving a shrub in autumn or winter, as long as it is not too cold or wet, will allow it to become established in time for its first summer.*

Staking a Shrub

In a well protected garden or in a border where a new shrub is surrounded by other supportive shrubs or plants, it may well be unnecessary to stake, but where the wind is likely to catch a shrub it is important to stake it until it is established.

SHORT AND TALL STAKING

The aim of staking a shrub is to allow the new roots to move out into the soil while anchoring the plant firmly. If the wind rocks the plant, the ball of soil that came with the plant is likely to move as well, severing the new roots that are trying to spread out into the surrounding soil.

The modern technique for staking trees and shrubs is to ensure that the base of the shrub is firmly anchored, preventing the rootball from moving, while the top is free to move in the wind, which will strengthen it. Thus, only a short stake is required, with a single tie about 25 cm (10 in) or so above the ground. If the shrub is top-heavy – for example, a standard rose – it is important to use a taller stake and tie it in two places, or the top of the shrub may well snap off. Unlike other forms of staking, this support should be left in place rather than removed once the shrub is established.

· Both short and tall staking is best done when first planting the shrub so that the roots can be seen. If the stake is knocked in afterwards it is likely to sever unseen roots. If it becomes necessary to stake a mature or already-planted shrub, use two stakes set some way out on either side of the shrub, with a crossbar to tie the stems to.

USEFUL SUPPORTS

A number of items can be used as stakes for shrubs. You can buy a variety of specially-designed plastic or wire supports from your local garden centre; alternatively, twiggy sticks pushed into the ground around a plant can be effective. Use short garden canes for fragile plants, tall canes for plants with tall, flowering stems and thicker pieces of wood for shrubs that need a stronger or more permanent means of support.

STAKING A STANDARD SHRUB

1 For a standard shrub, make sure you use a strong stake. It should be of a rot-resistant wood or one that has been treated with preservative. Firmly place the stake in the planting hole, knocking it into the soil so that it cannot move.

2 Plant the shrub, pushing the rootball up against the stake, so that the stem and stake are approximately 7.5–10 cm (3–4 in) apart.

3 Firm the soil down around the plant with the heel of your boot.

4 Although it is possible to use string, a proper rose or tree tie provides the best support. Fix the lower one 15 cm (6 in) above the soil.

5 Then fix the second tie near the top of the stake, just below the head of the standard shrub.

6 Water the ground around the plant thoroughly and mulch with a chipped bark or similar material.

Right: *Regularly check the ties, to make certain they are not too tight; otherwise they will begin to cut into the wood as the stems of the shrub increase in girth.*

Shrubs and Weather Problems

Weather, in particular winter weather, can cause problems for the shrub gardener. Throughout the year, winds can break branches of shrubs and, if there is any danger of this, shrubs should be firmly staked. If boughs or stems do break, cut them neatly back to a convenient point. If the wind is a constant problem, it becomes necessary to create a windbreak of some sort or shrubs will become permanently bent and, frequently, damaged.

PROTECTING AGAINST THE ELEMENTS

Frost can cause a lot of damage to shrubs, especially late or early frosts, which can catch new growth and flowers unexpectedly. General cold during the winter can be dealt with more easily, because it is relatively predictable: either cover the plants or plant them next to a wall, which will provide warmth and shelter.

Drought can be a problem, especially if it is not expected. Defend against drought when preparing the bed by incorporating plenty of moisture-retaining organic material. Once planted, shrubs benefit from a thick mulch, which will help hold the moisture in.

There are some plants that do not tolerate wet weather. Most plants with silver leaves, such as *Convolvulus cneorum* and lavenders prefer to grow in fairly dry conditions. Unfortunately there is little that can be done to protect such shrubs from the rain, although making their soil more free-draining by adding grit to the soil, or by growing them in well-drained containers usually helps.

Some shrubs prefer a shady position away from the sun. Many rhododendrons and azaleas, for example, prefer to be out of the hot sun. These can either be planted in the shade of a building or under trees or beneath taller shrubs.

WINDBREAKS

If there are perpetual problems with wind, it is essential to create some sort of windbreak. In the short term this can be plastic netting, but a more permanent solution is to create a living windbreak. A number of trees and shrubs can be used for this: *Leylandii* are often used, because they are one of the quickest-growing, but they are really best avoided for more suitable alternatives. They are thirsty and hungry plants that take a lot of the nutrients from the soil for some distance around their roots. They also continue growing rapidly past their required height.

It is best to get the windbreak established before the shrubs are planted but, if time is of the essence, plant them at the same time, shielding both from the winds with windbreak netting.

SHRUBS AND TREES FOR WINDBREAKS

Acer pseudoplatanus (sycamore)
Berberis darwinii
Buxus sempervirens (box)
Carpinus betulus (hornbeam)
Choisya ternata
Corylus avellana (hazel)
Cotoneaster simonsii
Crataegus monogyma (hawthorn)
Elaeagnus x ebbingei
Escallonia 'Langleyensis'
Euonymus japonicus 'Macrophyllus'
Fraxinus excelsior (ash)
Griselinia littoralis
Hippophaë rhamnoides (sea buckthorn)
Ilex (holly)
Ligustrum ovalifolium (privet)
Lonicera nitida (box-leaf honeysuckle)
Picea sitchensis (sitka spruce)
Pinus sylvestris (Scots pine)
Pittosporum tenuifolium
Prunus laurocerasus (cherry laurel)
Prunus lusitanica (Portuguese laurel)
Pyracantha (firethorn)
Rosmarinus officinalis (rosemary)
Sorbus aucuparia (rowan)
Tamarix (tamarisk)
Taxus baccata (yew)
Viburnum tinus (laurustinus)

Above: *Hedges are frequently used as windbreaks to protect the whole or specific parts of the garden. Whilst they are becoming established, they themselves may also need some protection, usually in the form of plastic netting. Here privet (*Ligustrum*) has been chosen.*

PROTECTING FROM WINTER COLD

1 Many shrubs, like this bay (*Laurus nobilis*) need some degree of winter protection. This shrub is in a container, but the same principles can be applied to free-standing shrubs. Insert a number of canes around the edge of the plant, taking care not to damage the roots.

2 Cut a piece of fleece, hessian (burlap) or bubble polythene (plastic) to the necessary size, making sure you allow for an overlap over the shrub and pot. Fleece can be bought as a sleeve, which is particularly handy for enveloping shrubs.

3 Wrap the protective cover around the plant, allowing a generous overlap. For particularly tender plants, use a double layer.

4 Tie the protective cover around the pot, or lightly around the shrub if it is in the ground. Fleece can be tied at the top as moisture can penetrate through, but if using plastic, leave it open for ventilation and watering.

5 Protecting with hessian (burlap) or plastic shade netting should be enough for most shrubs, but if a plant should require extra protection, wrap it in straw and then hold this in place with hessian or shade netting.

Above: *Late frost can ruin the flowering of a bush. This azalea has been caught on the top by the frost, but the sides were sufficiently sheltered to be unaffected. A covering of fleece would have given it complete protection.*

Right: *Lilac (Syringa) can be affected by late frosts which nip out the flowering buds preventing displays such as this.*

Caring for Climbers

Climbers are relatively maintenance-free and look after themselves, apart from one or two essential things. These essentials are, however, crucial not only to ensuring a good "performance" from your climbers, but also in making your garden safe for you and other users; so don't neglect these jobs, as they are important.

ESSENTIAL JOBS

The most important task is to be certain that the climber is well supported. Make regular checks that the main supports are still secure to the wall or that posts have not rotted or become loose in the wind.

Tie in any stray stems as they appear. If they are left, the wind may damage them. A worse situation can arise with thorned climbers, such as roses, whose thrashing stems may damage other plants or even passers-by. If they are not essential, cut off any stray stems to keep the climber neat and safe.

Throughout the flowering season, a climbing plant's appearance is improved by removing old flower heads. Dead-heading also prevents the plant from channelling vital resources into seed production, and thus frees energy for more flowering and growth.

WINTER PROTECTION

In winter, it may be important to protect the more tender climbers from the weather. Walls give a great deal of protection and may be sufficient for many plants but, even here, some plants may need extra protection if there is the possibility of a severe winter. One way is simply to drape hessian (burlap) or shade netting over the plant, to give temporary protection against frosts. For more prolonged periods, first protect the climber with straw and then cover this with hessian.

Keep an eye on climbers with variegated foliage, as some have the habit of reverting, that is, the leaves turn back to their normal green. If the stems bearing these leaves are not removed, the whole climber may eventually revert, losing its attractive foliage.

ROUTINE CARE

1 When vigorous climbers are grown against a house wall, they can become a nuisance once they have reached roof level.

4 Most climbers will produce stems that float around in space and that will need attention to prevent them being damaged or causing damage to other plants or passers-by. This *solanum* definitely needs some attention.

5 Regularly tie in any stray stems to the main supports. In some cases, it will be easier to attach them to other stems, rather than the supports. Always consider the overall shape of the climber and how you want to encourage it to grow in the future.

6 Sometimes it is better to cut off stray stems, either because there are already ample in that area or because they are becoming a nuisance. Trim them off neatly back to a bud or a branch. Sometimes, such stems will make useful cutting material from which to grow new plants.

2 At least once a year, cut back the new growth to below the level of the gutters and around the windows.

3 Dead-head regularly. If the dead flower is part of a truss, just nip out that flower; if the whole truss has finished, cut back the stem to a bud or leaf.

7 For light protection, especially against unseasonal frosts, hang shade netting or hessian (burlap) around the climber.

8 If the plant is against a wall, hang the shade netting or hessian from the gutter or from some similar support. This is a useful method of protecting new shoots and early flowers. For really tender plants, put a layer of straw around the stems of the climber and then hold it in place with a sheet of shade netting or hessian. Remove as soon as the plant begins to grow.

Above: *The overall effect of tying-in will be a neater and more satisfying shape. If possible, spread out the stems so that the climber looks fuller and less crowded.*

Providing Support for Climbers 1

When considering the choice and position of a climbing plant, it is important to take into account the method by which it climbs. While an ivy will support itself with modified roots on a brick wall, a rose, which is used to scrambling through bushes in the wild, will need to be tied to wires or trellis that has been attached to the wall.

CLIMBING HABITS

When buying a climbing plant, always consider the way it climbs and check that it is suitable for your purpose. If you want to cover a wall, and money is tight, an ivy is the best choice as it will cost no more than the plant, whereas the rose will also incur the price of the supporting structure. On the other hand, if you later want to paint the wall, it will be impossible to remove the ivy to do so, while a rose on a hinged or clipped trellis can be moved away from the wall to allow the operation to go ahead.

CLINGING CLIMBERS

True climbers are able to attach themselves to their supports. To do this, they have roots or modified roots that grip firmly on the surface of the support. They will attach themselves to any surface, including smooth ones such as glass and plastic. They need little attention, except for cutting them back from around windows and periodically cutting them off at the top of the wall so that they do not foul gutters or creep under tiles. If a wall is in good condition, there is little to fear from these climbers in terms of damage that they might inflict.

Above: Hydrangea anomala petiolaris *clings to wall surfaces by putting out modified roots.*

CLINGING CLIMBERS

Hedera canariensis (Canary Island ivy)
Hedera colchica (Persian ivy)
Hedera helix (common ivy)
Hydrangea anomala petiolaris (climbing hydrangea)
Parthenocissus henryana (Chinese Virginia creeper)
Parthenocissus quinquefolia (Virginia creeper)
Parthenocissus tricuspida (Boston ivy)

Right: *Clinging plants will cover any vertical surface without needing any support.*

CLIMBERS THAT USE TENDRILS

Many climbing plants have adapted themselves so that, although they do not cling to a smooth support, they can attach themselves to branches and other protrusions by means of tendrils. These are modified stems, or even leaves, which curl round the support.

Tendril plants will not climb up a wall unless there is already another plant on it or unless there is a mesh that they can attach themselves to. If a trellis or wires are used and the supporting strands are far apart, the stems will wave about until they are long enough to find something to which to cling; you may need to tie them in, to prevent them from breaking off. Closely woven mesh or another well-branched plant or tree provide the best supports for this type of climber.

CLIMBERS THAT USE TENDRILS

Campsis radicans
   (trumpet creeper)
Clematis
Cobaea scandens
   (cathedral bells)
Lathyrus (peas)
Mutisia
Vitis (vine)

Right: *The overall effect of a wall covered entirely by clematis is a mass of flower and foliage.*

Below: *Clematis puts out tendrils that entwine round a supporting structure, such as wire netting or another plant.*

Providing Support for Climbers 2

SCRAMBLING CLIMBERS

In the wild, apart from those that cling to cliffs, most climbers are supported by other plants. While some have adapted themselves to twine or use tendrils, the majority just push themselves up through the supporting plant, using its framework of branches and twigs as their support. Use this technique in the garden by allowing climbers to ramble up through shrubs and trees.

However, if the climbers are needed for a more formal situation, such as over a pergola or up a trellis or wall, artificial supports will be required. As the plants have no natural way of attaching themselves to wires or trellis, the gardener will have to tie them in with string or plant ties. This should be done at regular intervals, to ensure that the plant is well supported along its whole length.

TYPES OF TIES

There are various different materials for tying in stems. String is the most readily available and the cheapest. Use soft garden string for short-term (up to a year) tying in and tarred string for longer periods. Special twists made from thin wire covered with plastic "wings" are sold for garden use, although the version provided with plastic food bags is just as good.

Above: *Materials for tying in climbers* (left to right): *heavy-duty plastic tie; plastic twist tie; narrow plastic tie; tarred string; soft garden string.*

These are best used as temporary ties. Of more permanent use are plastic ties, which come in various sizes, from those suitable for holding stems, to those that will cope with small tree-trunks.

1 Use special lead-headed nails to attach the stems of scramblers to walls.

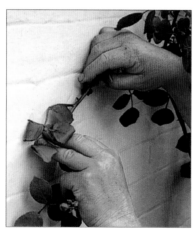

2 The malleable lead head can be wrapped around the stem to secure it.

Right: *Take advantage of scrambling climbers' natural habit of growing through other plants by growing a rose through an old apple tree.*

SCRAMBLING CLIMBERS

Akebia
Actinidia (some)
Bougainvillea
Eccremocarpus scaber (Chilean glory flower)
Fallopia baldschuanica (Russian vine)
Passiflora (passion-flower)
Plumbago capensis

Rhodochiton atrosanguineus
Rosa (rose)
Solanum (nightshade)
Thunbergia alata (black-eyed Susan)
Trachelospermum
Tropaeolum (nasturtium)
Vinca (periwinkle)

TWINING PLANTS

Some climbers twine their stems round the support as they grow. Plants that adopt this technique can be grown up poles or trellis, or through trees and shrubs. The stems automatically twist round their support, so little attention is required except to tie in any wayward shoots that might thrash around in the wind and get damaged.

Right: *The stems of twining climbers wind themselves round any support they can find as they grow, so, once you have provided the support, they will do the rest.*

Below: *Here, a hop has covered a metal arch with a shower of green leaves, supported by a mass of curling stems.*

TWINING CLIMBERS
Actinidia (some)
Humulus lupulus (hop)
Ipomoea (morning glory)
Lonicera (honeysuckle)
Phaseolus (climbing beans)

Above: Pyracantha *is a perfect wall shrub; it has flowers in the early summer and colourful berries in the autumn. Its branches are viciously thorned, making it a good burglar deterrent to plant on walls around windows.*

WALL SHRUBS

In gardening parlance, the term "climbing plants" is often liberally interpreted to include any plants that are grown up against walls. This can, in fact, include more or less any shrub. Generally, however, there are some shrubs that are best suited to this position, either because of their appearance or because they need the protection of the wall against the vagaries of the weather. Some are strong enough shrubs not to need support, except, perhaps, to be tied the wall to prevent them from being blown forward. Others need a more rigid support and should be tied into wires or a framework to keep them steady.

WALL SHRUBS
Abutilon
Azara
Carpenteria californica
Ceanothus (Californian lilac)
Cotoneaster
Euonymus fortunei
Magnolia
Pyracantha (firethorn)
Teucrium fruticans
   (shrubby germander)

PRUNING

Principles of Pruning

Pruning is the one thing that gardeners worry about more than anything else. The upshot is that many are frightened to do any pruning, feeling that it is probably best to leave things alone. While this may work with some plants, it is best to get into the habit of regularly checking all shrubs and climbers, and pruning those that need it. Certainly, the plants will benefit from this and will eventually deteriorate if left to their own devices.

BASIC PRUNING

There are several basic elements to pruning and taking them one step at a time makes the process easier. The first step is to remove all dead wood. This opens up the plant and makes it easier to see what is happening. The second is to remove any diseased wood. These are easy steps as it is not difficult to decide what to remove. The third stage is more difficult but becomes easier with practice. This is to remove any weak wood from the plant and to cut off stems that cross or rub others. Finally, to keep a plant vigorous it is important to encourage new growth. The way to do this is to remove a few of the oldest stems. Up to a third of the plant can be removed at any one time. Finally, check to see if any stems need removing to give the plant an attractive shape. Use sharp secateurs (pruners) or a saw for thicker branches, and keep your pruning cuts clean.

GOOD CUTS

1 A good pruning cut is made just above a strong bud, about 3 mm (⅛ in) above the bud. It should be a slanting cut, with the higher end above the bud. The bud should generally be outward bound from the plant rather than inward; the latter will throw its shoot into the plant, crossing and rubbing against others, which should be avoided. This is an easy technique and you can practise it on any stem.

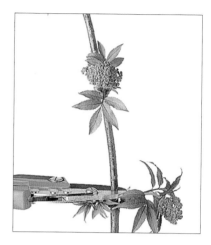

2 If the stem has buds or leaves opposite each other, make the cut horizontal, again about 3 mm (⅛ in) above the buds.

PRUNING THICKER BRANCHES

Most stems can be removed with secateurs (pruners), but thicker branches of large shrubs and rambling roses will require the use of a sharp pruning saw.

The major problem of cutting thicker stems is that they usually have a considerable weight. If cut straight through, this weight bends the stem before the cut has been completed, tearing the branch below the cut back to the main stem or trunk. The following technique avoids this. It is no longer considered necessary to paint large cuts to protect them.

1 Make a cut from the underside of the stem. Cut about half-way through or until the saw begins to bend as the weight of the stem closes the gap, pinching the saw.

2 Next, make a second cut from the upper edge of the stem, this time about 2.5 cm (1 in) away from the previous cut and further away from the main stem. The weight of the stem will then cause it to split across to the first cut so that the main part of the branch falls to the ground.

3 Make the third cut straight through the stem at the place to which you want to cut back. This should not tear the stem, because the weight has gone.

BAD CUTS

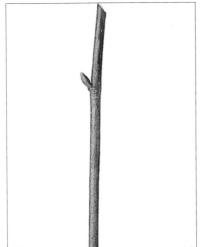

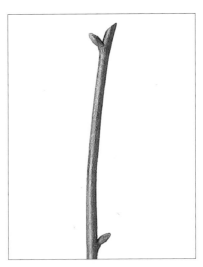

 Always use a sharp pair of secateurs (pruners). Blunt ones will produce a ragged or bruised cut, which is likely to introduce disease into the plant.

4 Do not cut too far above a bud. The piece of stem above the bud is likely to die back and the stem may well die back even further, causing the loss of the whole stem.

5 Do not cut too close to the bud otherwise the bud might be damaged by the secateurs (pruners) or disease might enter. Too close a cut is likely to cause the stem to die back to the next bud.

6 It is bad practice to slope the cut towards the bud as this makes the stem above the bud too long, which is likely to cause dieback. It also sheds rain on to the bud, which may cause problems.

DECIDING WHEN TO PRUNE

Perhaps the most difficult aspect of pruning is deciding when to do it. Gardeners worry that if they do it at the wrong time they might kill the plant. This is possible but unlikely. The worst that usually happens is that you cut off all the stems that will produce the year's flowers and so you miss a season. As a rule of thumb, most shrubs need to be pruned immediately after they have flowered, so that they have time to produce new mature stems by the time they need to flower again.

Above: Rosa 'Bantry Bay' climbing up a metal obelisk. Roses need to be dead-headed and pruned to keep them at their best. If you don't care for them properly, the plants become very straggly and flowering diminishes.

Above: Wisterias are grown for their magnificent flowers and are suitable for growing against walls, buildings and even trees. They also make good climbers for pergolas. They should be pruned after flowering and again in the winter. This is Japanese wisteria (Wisteria floribunda).

Pruning Shrubs

Apart from pruning a shrub to improve its shape, you may also need to prune out potential problems, such as damage and disease. Once a year, thoroughly check whether your plant needs attention.

CUTTING OUT DEAD WOOD

Cut out all dead wood from the shrub. This can be done at pruning time or at any other time of year when you can see dead material. Cut the dead wood out where it reaches live wood, which may be where the shoot joins a main stem or at the base of the plant. If the shrub is a large, tangled one, it may be necessary to cut out the dead branches bit by bit, as the short sections may be easier to remove than one long piece, especially if the stems have thorns that catch on everything.

CUTTING OUT CROSSING STEMS

Most shrubs grow out from a central point, with their branches arching gracefully outwards. However, sometimes a shoot will grow in towards the centre of the bush, crossing other stems in its search for light on the other side of the shrub. While there is nothing intrinsically wrong with this growth pattern, it is best to remove such branches as they will soon crowd the other branches and will often chafe against them, rubbing off the bark from the stem.

CUTTING OUT CROSSING STEMS

█ Cut out the stems while they are still young and free from damage and disease. Using secateurs (pruners), cut the stem at its base where it joins the main branch.

CUTTING OUT DIEBACK

█ Tips of stems often die back, especially those that have carried bunches of flowers. Another cause is the young growth at the tip of shoots being killed by frost. If this die-back is not cut out, it can eventually kill off the whole shoot. Even if die-back proceeds no further it is still unsightly and the bush looks much tidier without these dead shoots. Cut the shoot back into good wood, just above a strong bud.

CUTTING OUT DISEASED OR DAMAGED WOOD

█ Cut any diseased or damaged wood back to sound wood, just above a strong bud. The wood is usually quite easy to spot. It may not be dead yet but still in the process of turning brown or black.

HARD PRUNING

1 There are a few shrubs – buddlejas are the main example – which benefit from being cut hard back each spring, much improving the foliage. Elders (*Sambucus*) and the purple smoke bush (*Cotinus*) are best treated in this way. *Rosa glauca* also responds very well to this type of pruning.

2 Cut the shoots right back almost to the ground, making the cuts just above an outward-facing bud and leaving little more than a stump. It may seem a little drastic, but the shrubs will quickly grow again in the spring. If they are not cut back, they become very leggy and do not make such attractive bushes.

3 Several plants that have attractive coloured bark in the winter are best cut to the ground in the spring.

4 So by the following winter, new attractive shoots will be displayed. The various coloured-stemmed *Rubus*, such as *R. cockburnianus* as well as some of the dogwoods (*Cornus* 'sibirica') and willows (*Salix*) are good candidates for this treatment.

DEAD-HEADING

1 Regular dead-heading will keep the shrub looking tidy and will also help promote further flowering. Roses, in particular, appreciate regular attention. Cut the flowering stems back to a bud or stem division.

Right: *The flowering on roses will always be improved if they are regularly dead-headed. This vigorous, multi-coloured rose is 'Miss Pam Ayres'.*

Basic Pruning for Climbers

The basics of pruning are not at all difficult, although the task of tackling a huge climber that covers half the house may seem rather daunting. Break it into three logical stages to make it more manageable.

THREE-STAGE PRUNING

The first pruning stage is to remove all dead wood. These stems are now of no use and only make the climber congested. Moreover, clearing these first will enable you to see where to prune next.

The second stage is to remove diseased and dying wood. This type of wood is usually obvious and should be taken out before it affects the rest of the plant.

The third stage is to remove some of the older wood. This has the effect of causing the plant to throw up new growth, which ensures the plant's continuing survival and keeps it vigorous, producing plenty of healthy flowers.

DISPOSAL OF WASTE

How to get rid of the mass of waste material pruned from climbing plants has always been a problem. The traditional method was to burn it but this is a waste of organic material and creates environmental problems, especially in urban areas. The best way is to shred it (avoiding diseased material). The waste is then composted for a couple of months and then returned to the beds as a valuable mulch. If you do not own a shredder then perhaps it is possible to borrow or hire one. Some local authorities run recycling schemes in which they compost all organic garden waste for reuse. The last resort is to take it to the local refuse tip. Do not dump waste in the countryside.

PRUNING OUT DISEASED WOOD

1 Remove any diseased wood, cutting it back to a point on the stem where the wood is again healthy. If the cut end shows that the wood is still diseased on the inside of the stem, cut back further still.

REMOVING OLD WOOD

3 Up to a third of the old wood should be removed, to encourage the plant to produce new growth. If possible, cut some of this out to the base; also remove some of the upper stems, cutting them back to a strong growing point.

PRUNING OUT DEAD WOOD

1 Most climbers produce a mass of dead wood that has to be removed so that the plant does not become congested. Dead wood is normally quite clearly differentiated from the live wood, by its colour and lack of flexibility.

2 Thin out the dead wood, removing it in sections, if necessary, so that the remaining stems are not damaged when it is pulled out.

TYING IN

1 Tie in the remaining stems, spreading them out rather than tying them in a tight column of stems. If possible, spread at least some of the stems horizontally: this will not only produce a better wall or trellis cover but also encourage flowering.

Right: *At their peak, roses are amongst the loveliest of climbing plants. Here the rambling* Rosa *'Excelsa' is seen climbing up a pillar.*

Pruning Climbing Roses

Roses climbing through a tree are usually left to their own devices, because they are difficult to get at; any roses climbing up a wall, trellis or pergola, however, should be regularly pruned, not only to remove dead and old wood but also to keep them vigorous and flowering well. Unpruned roses become old before their time, their flowering decreases and they look scruffy.

ONCE-FLOWERING CLIMBING ROSES

As with most woody plants, the time to prune is immediately after flowering. For once-flowering climbing roses, this normally means in midsummer.

However, if you want to see the rose's colourful hips in the autumn, leave the pruning and wait until the birds come and remove the hips or until the fruits have lost their brilliance and are no longer attractive.

1 Pruning in summer means that the plant will be in full leaf and growth. Although this may seem a daunting task to tackle, it makes it easy to see what is dead and what is alive. If possible, it is often easier to prune climbing roses by removing them from their supports and laying the stems on the ground.

2 First, remove all dead main stems and side-shoots. Cut these right back to living wood; if they are difficult to remove, take them out in sections rather than all at once. Next, remove one or two of the oldest stems. This will promote new vigorous shoots. Cut back some of the older wood growing at the top of the plant to a vigorous new shoot lower down. Do not remove more than a third of the old wood, unless you want to reduce the size of the climber drastically.

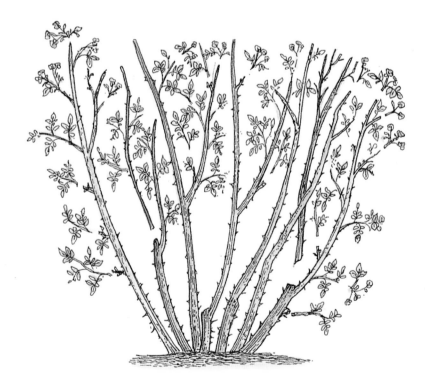

Above: *Cut out some of the older stems as soon as they have flowered, cutting back to a strong growing point, either at the base or higher up.*

3 Tie in the remaining shoots, if they are loose. Any young shoots that come from the base will need to be regularly tied in as they grow, to prevent them from thrashing around.

4 Once secure, prune back any of the shorter side shoots to three or four buds. At the same time, cut back the tips of any new main shoots that have flowered, to a sound bud.

REPEAT-FLOWERING ROSES

There are now many roses that continue to flower throughout the summer and well into the autumn. It is obviously not desirable to prune these during the summer or you will lose the later flowers. Light pruning, restricted to removing dead flowers and any dead wood, can be carried out throughout the summer, but the main pruning is best left until the winter, when the rose is dormant. It is easier to see where to prune, too.

Below: *The abundance of flowers on Rosa 'Alba maxima' makes it impossible to prune in summer.*

REPEAT-FLOWERING ROSES

'Agatha Christie' (pink)
'Aloha' (pink)
'Bantry Bay' (pink)
'Casino' (yellow)
'Coral Dawn' (pink)
'Danse du Feu' (red)
'Gloire de Dijon' (buff)
'Golden Showers' (yellow and cream)
'Handel' (white and pink)
'Parkdirektor Riggers' (red)
'Pink Perpétue' (pink)
'Royal Gold' (yellow)
'Schoolgirl' (orange)
'Summer Wine' (pink)

1 One advantage of pruning in the winter is that the leaves are missing, giving you a clearer picture of what you are doing. The structure of the rose, in particular, is more obvious.

2 First, remove any dead or diseased wood, cutting right back into living wood. Next, take out a few of the oldest shoots from the base, to encourage new growth for a compact shape.

3 If any flowering shoots remain on the tips of the stems, cut these out, taking the stem back to a sound bud. The side shoots can be shortened to about half their length. Tie in all loose stems.

4 In the summer, dead-head the roses as the flowers go over. This not only makes the climber tidier but promotes further flowering. With tall climbers, however, this may be impractical!

Pruning Rambling Roses

Ramblers only flower once during the summer. These flowers are formed on old wood produced during the previous season, so it is important to prune as soon as possible after flowering. This allows plenty of time for new shoots to grow, ready for next season's crop of flowers.

1 Because they are pruned in summer, the plants look congested and it is difficult to see what to prune. If possible, untie the shoots from their support and lay them out on the ground, so that you can see what you are doing. If this is not possible, remove the stems that need cutting out in sections and keep checking as you go.

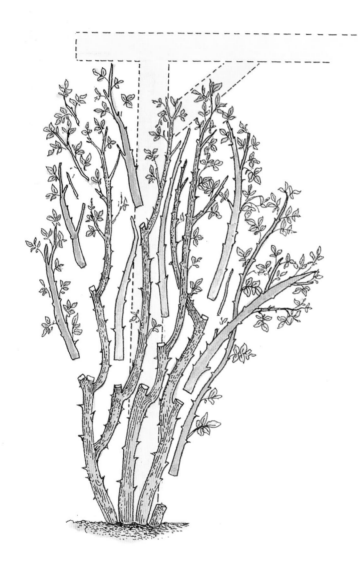

Above: *Remove older stems as soon as they have flowered, cutting back to a strong growing point, either at the base or higher up.*

2 Remove any diseased, dead or dying stems at the base. This may well reduce the rambler considerably and make subsequent pruning easier.

3 Cut out to the base any wood that has flowered during the summer. This should only leave new growth. However, if there is not much new growth, leave some of the older stems intact, to flower again the following season.

4 If you have retained any older shoots, cut back their side shoots to two or three buds. Tie in all remaining shoots. If possible, tie these to horizontal supports, to encourage flowering and new growth.

BARE AT THE BASE?

Sometimes rambler roses are reluctant to produce new shoots from the base of the plant. In that case, if there are new stems arising higher up the plant, cut back the old ones to this point.

Right: Rosa 'Bobby James' is a vigorous rambling rose that needs regular pruning to keep it flowering well. Gloves should be worn as it has vicious thorns.

Pruning Clematis

Many gardeners worry about pruning clematis: the task seems complex, and is made more difficult because different clematis plants require different treatment. While this is true, the actual treatment is quite simple and soon becomes routine. If you grow a lot of clematis, keep a record of which plant needs what treatment. Alternatively, attach a label to each one, stating what type it is. This will make pruning very much easier.

Above: *There is always room to grow yet another clematis. Here the double* C. viticella *'Purpurea Plena Elegans' climbs over a wooden shed. For pruning it belongs to Group 3.*

CLEMATIS PRUNING GROUPS

There are three groups of clematis, as far as pruning is concerned. Most clematis catalogues or plant labels state what type each belongs to. However, it is possible to work it out. Small-flowered spring varieties such as *Clematis montana* belong to Group 1. Several of the early-flowering species also belong to this pruning group.

Group 2 consists of large-flowered clematis that bloom in early to midsummer, on old wood produced during the previous year.

Group 3 are the large-flowered climbing plants that bloom later in the summer on new wood produced during the spring.

PRUNING GROUPS FOR SOME OF THE MORE POPULAR CLEMATIS

C. 'Abundance'	3	C. macropetala	1
C. alpina	1	C. 'Madame Julia Correvon'	3
C. 'Barbara Jackman'	2	C. 'Marie Boisselot'	2
C. 'Bill Mackenzie'	3	C. 'Miss Bateman'	2
C. cirrhosa	1	C. montana	1
C. 'Comtesse de Bouchard'	3	C. 'Mrs Cholmondeley'	2
C. 'Daniel Deronda'	2	C. 'Nelly Moser'	2
C. 'Duchess of Albany'	3	C. 'Perle d'Azur'	3
C. 'Elsa Späth'	2	C. 'Royal Velours'	3
C. 'Ernest Markham'	2	C. 'Star of India'	2
C. 'Etoile Violette'	3	C. tangutica	3
C. 'Hagley Hybrid'	3	C. tibetana (orientalis)	3
C. 'Jackmanii'	3	C. 'The President'	2
C. 'Lasurstern'	2	C. viticella	3
C. 'Little Nell'	3	C. 'Vyvyan Pennell'	2

WHICH GROUP?

Does it flower in spring or early summer and have relatively small flowers?

Yes = It is probably Group 1.
No = Go to the next question.

Does it bloom in early or midsummer, possibly with a few flowers later, and are the flowers large?

Yes = It is probably Group 2.
No = Go to the next question.

Does it flower from mid- or late summer and into autumn?

Yes = It is probably Group 3.
No = There is an area of doubt, so consult a clematis expert or specialist nursery if you cannot find the variety listed on this page.

Pruning Group 1 Clematis

This group consists mainly of small-flowered clematis. Most flower early in the year, usually in spring, such as *C. montana*, although *C. cirrhosa* flowers in winter. This is the easiest group to deal with as you can, generally, leave them to their own devices, resorting to pruning only when they grow too big and need to be cut back.

1 Keep the climber looking healthy by removing any dead growth. This will help to reduce the bulk and weight of the climber, which can become considerable over the years.

2 If space is limited, remove some stems immediately after flowering. Cut them back to where they join a main shoot. Stray shoots that are thrashing around can also be removed.

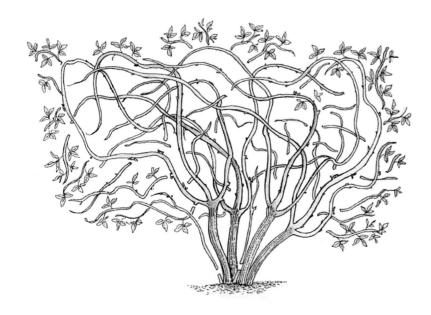

Above: *Group 1 clematis only need pruning when they outgrow their space. Just cut out sufficient branches to reduce congestion, and take those that encroach beyond their space back to their point of origin.*

Right: *Typical of Group 1 is this* C. montana.

Pruning Group 2 Clematis

Group 2 clematis need a little more care and attention to make them flower well. If they are left alone, they become very leggy, so that all the flowering is taking place at the top of the plant, out of view. The basic pruning goal is to reduce the number of shoots while leaving in a lot of the older wood. You can do this immediately after flowering but it is more usual to wait until late winter, before the clematis comes into growth.

1 First, cut out all dead or broken wood. If this is tangled up, cut it out a little at a time, so that it does not damage the wood that is to remain.

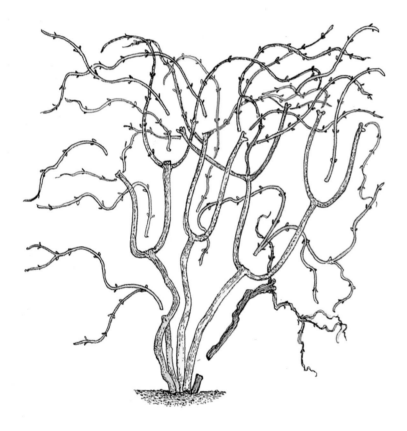

Above: *After cutting out all the dead, damaged or weak growth, remove any wood that is making the clematis congested, cutting back to a pair of buds.*

2 Cut out all weak growths, to a strong bud. If the climber is still congested, remove some of the older stems.

3 Do not remove too much material or the flowering for the following season will be reduced. If a plant has been cut back too drastically, it will often flower much later in the season than usual, and is likely to produce smaller flowers.

4 Spread out the remaining shoots, so that the support is well covered. If left to find their own way, the shoots will grow up in a column.

Right: *Correctly pruned, Group 2 clematis, such as this* Clematis *'Niobe', will provide an abundance of flowers throughout the summer.*

Pruning Group 3 Clematis

Once you have recognized that you have one of the plants that constitute this group, the actual process of pruning is very straightforward. The flowers appear on wood that grows during the current year, so all the previous year's growth can be cut away. These make good plants to grow through early-flowering shrubs, because the shrub will have finished blooming by the time that the new growth on the clematis has begun to cover its branches.

1 Once Group 3 clematis become established, they produce a mass of stems at the base. If they are allowed to continue growing naturally, the flowering area gets higher and higher, leaving the base of the plant bare.

2 In mid- to late winter cut back all the shoots to within 1 m (3 ft), and preferably much less, of the ground. If the clematis is growing through a shrub, carefully untangle the stems from the shrub's branches and remove them.

3 Cut the stems back to a sound pair of plump buds. As the wood gets older, so the cuts for subsequent years are likely to get higher, but there is always plenty of new growth from the base, which should be cut low down.

4 Once cut back, the clematis looks quite mutilated but the buds will soon produce new shoots and new growth will also appear from the base; by midsummer, the support will, once again, be covered with new growth bearing a profusion of flowers.

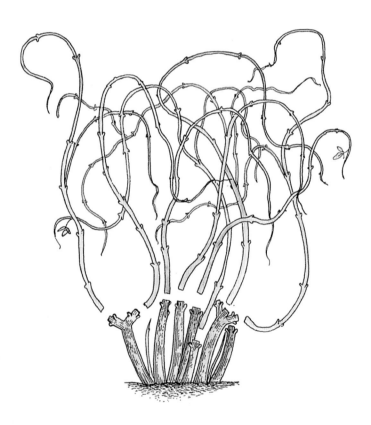

Above: *Group 3 clematis should have all the growth cut back in midwinter to the first pair of sound buds above the ground.*

Pruning Wisterias

Gardeners often complain that their wisteria never flowers. One of the reasons that this might happen is that they never prune the climber and consequently all the plant's energy seems to go in producing ever-expanding, new growth rather than flowers. Gardeners often seem reluctant to prune wisteria, possibly because it is usually done in two stages, one in summer and the other in winter. However, it is not at all difficult once you know the idea behind it. For the first few years allow the wisteria to grow out to form the basic framework, removing any unwanted stems.

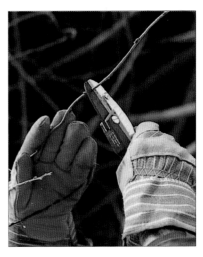

1 During the spring and early summer, the wisteria produces long, wispy new growth that looks like tendrils. Around midsummer, this new growth should be trimmed back, leaving only four leaves on each shoot. Any shoots that are required to extend the range or shape of the wisteria should be left unpruned.

2 From early to midwinter, cut back the summer-pruned shoots even further, to about half their length, leaving two to three buds on each shoot. This generally means that the previous season's growth will now be about 7.5 cm (3 in) long, thus drastically reducing the overall growth rate of the climber.

Above: *Cut back the new growth each summer to about four leaves and reduce this even further with a winter pruning.*

Right: *All the effort is worthwhile when you achieve a display as stunning as this one.*

PROPAGATION

Advice on Seed

Growing a plant from seed is one of the easiest methods of propagation as well as a satisfying one. There is great pleasure to be had from seeing a tiny seed develop into a soaring plant that climbs up the side of a house, or seeing a fully mature shrub, perhaps covered in flowers, and knowing that you grew it from a small seed. Growing shrubs from seed requires more patience than propagating climbers: many shrubs take a number of years between sowing and growing to reach flowering size.

PROPAGATION

Seed can be obtained from seed merchants, friends or one of the many seed exchanges run by horticultural clubs. More exotic and rare seed can be bought from various seed-collecting expeditions that advertise their products in specialist gardening magazines.

Sow the seed as soon as you get it in one of the many soil mixes available (see the opposite page for details of their various properties). For climbers, stand the pot in a sheltered position outside or in a greenhouse or heated propagator for faster germination. For shrubs, put the pots out in an open, shady place where they experience whatever the weather throws at them. Keep them watered in dry weather, but do not cover them in cold weather, as the cold will often help over-ride any dormancy that there might be in the seed, which would prevent it from germinating. Bear in mind that germination might take a couple of years, so be patient. Seed that is encased in berries

needs to have the fleshy part removed before it is sown.

Unless you want to grow a huge number of one particular variety of shrub or climber, a 9 cm (3½ in) pot is a large enough container, as this will produce up to twenty seedlings.

1 Fill the pot right up to the rim with compost (soil mix). Settle it by tapping it sharply on the bench or table. Very lightly press down and level the surface with the base of a similar sized pot. Do not press too hard. The level of the compost should now be below the rim of the pot.

PLANTING SEED IN POTS

2 Shrub and climber seeds are, on the whole, quite large and can be sown individually. Space them out evenly on the surface of the compost (soil mix). Do not be tempted to overfill the pot. If you have a lot of seed, use two pots. Smaller seed can be scattered over the surface but, again, do not overcrowd and ensure that they are well spaced.

3 Cover the seed and compost (soil mix) with a layer of fine grit, which should be at least 1 cm (½ in) thick. This will make it easier to water the pot evenly as well as making it easier to remove any weeds, moss or liverwort that may start to grow on the surface. It also provides a well drained area around the rot-prone neck of the emerging seedling.

4 Before you do anything else, label the pot. One pot of seed looks exactly like any other pot and they will soon get into a muddle if the pots are not labelled. Include the name of the plant and the date on which you sowed the seed on the labels. The source of the seed can also be useful additional information. Some gardeners like to keep a "sowing book", in which they record complete details of sowing and what happens afterwards, such as germination time and survival rates.

5 Water the pot with a watering can with a fine rose (nozzle). Place pots containing shrub seed in the open, but shielded from the sun; climber seeds should stand in a sheltered position or in a warmer atmosphere for faster growth. Do not let the compost dry out.

PRICKING OUT

Once the seedlings have germinated, it is important to keep them growing on. Water them regularly and pot them on as soon as possible. This is important, as the sowing compost (soil mix) is not very rich in nutrients and the seedlings will soon become starved. In addition, if the seedlings are left in the pot for any length of time they will become overcrowded and very drawn and spindly. Most seedlings are best pricked out into individual plant pots rather than seed trays.

Use a good potting compost (soil mix) that does not contain too much fertilizer. You can use a stronger one when you pot the seedlings on at a later stage.

SEED AND POTTING COMPOST

Seed and potting composts (soil mixes) come in soilless and soil-based forms, and which you use will be a matter of personal preference. Seed seems happy in either but different composts (soil mixes) seem to suit different regimes. Try some of each to see which suits.

Soilless composts (planting mixes) are mainly based on fibrous material such as peat or a peat substitute like coir. They are light-weight, moisture-retentive, easy to over-water and yet difficult to re-wet if allowed to dry out. Soil-based composts (soil mixes) are heavier, well-drained, difficult to over-water, but absorb water easily when dry.

PRICKING OUT SEEDLINGS

1 Fill the bottom of enough clean pots with a good potting compost (soil mix). Invert the pot containing the seedlings and tap it on the bench or table, so that the contents come out in one lump. Gently divide the root-ball and ease a seedling away from it, making certain not to tear the roots. Hold the seedling only by the leaves and not by the stem or roots.

2 Still holding the seedling by a leaf, suspend it over the centre of one of the pots, resting your hand on the edge of the pot to steady it. With the other hand, gently fill the pot with compost (soil mix).

3 Gently tap the pot on the table to settle the compost (soil mix), and lightly firm it down with your fingers, levelling off the surface. Add a 1 cm (½ in) layer of fine grit to the surface. Label the pot immediately. Repeat the process for all the other seedlings.

4 Water the seedlings, either from below in a water bath or from above with a watering can with a fine rose. Place the pots in a shady spot, preferably under a closed cold frame for a few days and then slowly open the lights to harden the plants off.

Taking Shrub Cuttings

Raising new plants from seed is easy but takes rather a long time. The length of time between propagation and having a plant ready to go outside can be reduced by taking cuttings instead. Important as this may be, the real advantage of taking cuttings is that the resulting offspring are identical to their parent. Plants from seed, on the other hand, vary, sometimes so minutely that you cannot tell them apart but sometimes by a large amount: the leaves may be a different colour or the flowers a different size. Sometimes the variation is a welcome one and you obtain a new plant that is worth having, but, on the whole, the opposite seems to be the case. With cuttings, however, you always know what you are going to get.

SEMI-RIPE AND HARDWOOD CUTTINGS

Taking cuttings is a simple procedure. A heated propagator helps but it is not essential; you can use a simple plastic bag as a cover, to create an enclosed environment. Hardy plants will root outside, but they will need a cold frame to protect them.

There are two basic types of cuttings: semi-ripe and hardwood. The semi-ripe cuttings are taken from the current year's wood. They are taken from midsummer onwards at a point when the soft tips of the shoots are beginning to harden and are no longer quite as flexible. They are often just changing colour from a light green to a darker one.

Hardwood cuttings are taken from the shrubs at the shoot's next stage, when it has become hard, ready to experience the frosts of winter. These are taken from autumn onwards.

In both cases, always choose healthy shoots that are free of

disease or damage. Avoid any that are covered with insect pests. Aphids, for example, transmit viral diseases as well as weakening stems. Avoid shoots which have become drawn and spindly by growing towards the light and have a long distance between leaves. Usually, the shoots near the top of the bush are better than those towards the base, where they are starved of light. Put all cuttings in a plastic bag as soon as you take them, to stop them drying out.

The compost (soil mix) to use is a cutting compost, which can be readily purchased. However, it is easy to make your own as it consists of 50 per cent (by volume) sharp sand and 50 per cent peat or peat substitute. Instead of sand, you can use vermiculite.

The cuttings are ready to be potted on once they have rooted. Usually new growth starts on the stem, but if not carefully dig up the root ball and check for new roots.

TAKING SEMI-RIPE SHRUB CUTTINGS

1 Choose a stem that is not too flexible and is just turning woody where it joins last year's hard growth. Cut it just above a bud and put the whole stem into a plastic bag. Collect several stems.

2 Cut the stem below a bud and make the top cut just above a leaf 10 cm (4 in) above the base leaf. Cleanly remove the bottom leaves with a sharp knife, leaving only the top leaves.

3 Dip the base of the stem into a rooting powder or liquid. This will help the cutting to root and also protect it, as the powder or liquid contains a fungicide. Tap the stem to remove the excess.

4 Make a trench in the compost (soil mix) with a small object and place the cutting in, making sure the base is in contact with the compost.

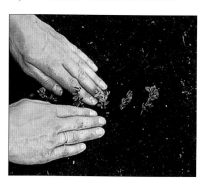

5 Firm the compost around the stem, so that there are no air pockets. Continue planting the other cuttings, making sure they are well spaced.

6 Water the compost and spray the leaves with a copper fungicide. Label the plant. If using a pot, place it in a propagator or cover with a plastic bag. If outside, place under a cold frame.

TAKING HARDWOOD CUTTINGS

In many ways, hardwood cuttings are even easier to take than semi-ripe ones, but they will take longer to root.

Once you have planted the cuttings, leave them in the ground until at least the next autumn, by which time they should have rooted. They will often produce leaves in the spring but this is not necessarily a sign that they have rooted.

Once you think they have rooted, test by digging one up. If they have, they can be transferred to pots or a nursery bed where they can be grown on to form larger plants before being moved to a permanent position.

1 Cut about 30 cm (12 in) of straight, fully ripened (hard) stem from a shrub.

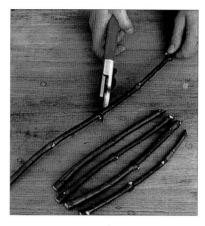

2 Trim the stem off just below a leaf joint and remove any soft tip, so that the eventual length is about 23 cm (9 in) long. Remove any leaves.

3 Although a rooting hormone is not essential, it should increase the success rate, especially with plants that are difficult to root. Moisten the bases of the cuttings in water.

4 Choose a sheltered, shady spot in the garden and dig a slit in the ground with a spade. If the soil is heavy dig out a narrow trench and fill it with either cutting compost or sharp sand.

5 Insert the cuttings in the ground, leaving the top 7 cm (3 in) or so of the stem above ground.

6 Firm the soil around the cuttings to eliminate pockets of air that would cause the cuttings to dry out. Once the cuttings have rooted, dig them up and pot them on in the normal way. This will normally be the following autumn.

SHRUBS TO TRY

These are just some shrubs that will root from hardwood cuttings:

Aucuba japonica (spotted laurel)
Buddleja (butterfly bush)
Cornus (dogwood)
Forsythia
Ligustrum
Philadelphus (mock orange)
Ribes (currant)
Rosa
Salix (willow)
Sambucus (elder)
Spiraea
Viburnum (deciduous species)

Climbers from Cuttings

While using seed to increase plants is a simple procedure, it has the disadvantage that the resulting plant may not be like its parent, because not all plants will come "true" from seed. Seed-raised plants may vary in flower or leaf colour, in the size of the plant and in many other ways. When you propagate from cuttings, however, the resulting plant is identical in all ways to its parent (it is, effectively, a clone).

TAKING CUTTINGS

Taking cuttings is not a difficult procedure and nearly all climbers can easily be propagated in this way without much trouble. It is not necessary to have expensive equipment, although, if you intend to produce a lot of new plants, a heated propagator will make things much easier.

The most satisfactory method of taking cuttings is to take them from semi-ripe wood, that is, from this year's growth that is firm to the touch but still flexible and not yet hard and woody. If the shoot feels soft and floppy, it is too early to take cuttings. The best time for taking such cuttings is usually from mid- to late summer.

When taking cuttings it is vital that you always choose shoots that are healthy: they should be free from diseases and pests and not be too long between nodes (leaf joints). This usually means taking the cuttings from the top of the climber, where it receives plenty of light.

Do not take cuttings from any suckers that may rise from the base of the plant; if the climber was grafted on to a different rootstock, you might find that you have propagated another plant entirely.

CHOOSING COMPOST (SOIL MIX)

Specialist cutting compost (soil mix) can be purchased from most garden centres and nurseries. However, it is very simple to make your own. A half and half mix, by volume, of peat (or peat substitute) and sharp sand is all that is required. Alternatively, instead of sharp sand, use vermiculite.

1 Choose a healthy shoot that is not too spindly. Avoid stems that carry a flower or bud, as these are difficult to root. Cut the shoot longer than is required and trim it to size later. Put the shoot in a polythene (plastic) bag, so that it does not wilt while waiting for your attention.

2 Remove the shoot from the bag when you are ready to deal with it. Cut at an angle just below a leaf joint (node). Use a sharp knife, so that the cut is clean and not ragged.

3 Trim off the rest of the stem just above a leaf, so that the cutting is about 10 cm (4 in) long. For long-jointed climbers, this may be the next leaf joint up; for others there may be several leaves on the cutting.

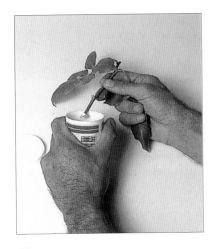

4 Trim off all leaves except the upper one or pair. Cut the leaves off right against the stem, so that there are no snags. However, be careful not to damage the stem. Dip the base of the cutting into a rooting compound, either powder or liquid. This will not only promote rooting but also help protect the cutting against fungal attack.

5 Fill a 9 cm (3½ in) pot with cutting compost (soil mix) and insert the cuttings round the edge. Pushing them into the compost removes the rooting powder and damages the stems, so make a hole with a small dibber or pencil. Several cuttings can be put into one pot but do not overcrowd. Tap the pot on the bench, to settle the compost. Water gently. Label the pot.

6 If a propagator is available, place the pot in it and close the lid so that fairly high humidity and temperature are maintained. A less expensive alternative is to put the pot into a polythene (plastic) bag, with its sides held away from the leaves. Put it in a warm, light, but not sunny, position.

7 After a few weeks, the base of the cutting will callus over and roots will begin to appear. Carefully invert the pot, while supporting the compost with your other hand. Remove the pot and examine the roots. Once the roots are well developed, pot the cuttings up individually. Put the pot back in the propagator if roots are only just beginning to appear.

INTERNODAL CUTTINGS

A few plants, of which clematis is the main example, are propagated from internodal cuttings. The procedure is the same as for conventional cuttings, except that the bottom cut is through the stem, between two pairs of leaves, rather than under the bottom pair.

Right: *Your cuttings will eventually grow into hearty plants like this 'Rosa Cedric Morris'. These rambling roses can be grown through a large tree, as long as the tree is strong enough to take all the extra weight.*

Layering Shrubs

Layering is a good way of producing the odd few extra plants without a propagator. It is a useful method of producing one or two plants from a bush that somebody might want, without all the bother of what might be termed "formal" propagation. It is not a difficult technique and, after the initial work, nothing has to be done until the new plant is ready for transplanting – and it does not require any special equipment.

FOLLOWING NATURE

Basically, layering is simply persuading the plant to do what it often does in the wild (and in the garden, for that matter) and that is to put down roots where a branch or stem touches the ground. Encourage this by burying the stem and holding it in position with a peg or stone, so that the wind does not move it and sever any roots that are forming. It is as simple as that. Frequently, you will find that nature has already done it for you and a search around the base of many shrubs will reveal one or more layers that have already rooted on their own.

While layering might sound a casual way of propagating, it is a good one to try if you have difficulty in rooting cuttings. Being connected to the parent plant, the shoot still has a supply of nutrients and is, therefore, still very much alive, whereas a cutting may well have used up all its reserves and died before it has had a chance to put down roots. A layer is also far less prone to being killed off by a fungal disease.

DIVISION

Shrubs suitable for division produce multiple stems from below the ground or increase by suckering or running (self-layering). At any time between autumn and early spring, dig up one of the suckers or a portion of the shrub, severing it from the parent plant with secateurs (pruners) or a sharp knife and replant or pot up the divided portion. Suitable shrubs include *Arctostaphylos, Calluna, Clerodendrum bungei, Cornus alba, C. canadensis, Erica, Gaultheria, Holodiscolor, Kerria, Leucothoe, Mahonia, Nandina, Pachysandra, Rubus, Sarcococca* and *Sorbus reducta.*

1 Choose a stem that will reach the ground without breaking and prepare the ground beneath it. In most cases, the native soil will be satisfactory but if it is heavy clay add some potting compost (potting soil) to improve its texture.

2 Trim off any side-shoots or leaves. Dig a shallow hole and bend the shoot down into it.

3 To help hold the shoot in place, peg it down with a piece of bent wire.

4 Fill in the hole and cover it with a stone. In many cases, the stone will be sufficient to hold the layer in place and a peg will not be required. The stone will also help to keep the area beneath it moist.

5 It may take several months, or even years, for shrubs that are hard to propagate to layer but, eventually, new shoots will appear and the layer will have rooted. Sever it from its parent and pot it up into a container.

6 If the roots are well developed, transfer the layer directly to its new site.

IMPROVING ROOTING

Although it is not essential, rooting can be improved with difficult subjects by making a slit in the underside of the stem at a point where it will be below ground. This slit can be propped open with a thin sliver of wood or a piece of grit. This cut interrupts the passage of hormones along the stem and they accumulate there, helping to promote more rapid rooting.

If several plants are required, it is quite feasible to make several layers on the same shoot, allowing the stem to come above the surface between each layer. This is known as "serpentine layering".

Above: *Rhododendrons frequently self-layer in the wild and may also do so in the garden, but the prudent gardener always deliberately makes a few layers just in case a visiting friend takes a liking to one of the varieties that he grows.*

Layering Climbers

Layering is a simple technique, useful for propagating plants that are difficult to root from cuttings. It can be a slow process: occasionally, some plants can take several years to root. If one or two layers can be laid down at regular intervals, however, you should have a continuous supply of new plants at your disposal.

TIMING LAYERING

Layering can be carried out at any time of year. The time taken for roots to appear on the chosen stem depends on various factors and varies considerably from one type of plant to another. Usually, growth appearing from the area of the layer indicates that it has rooted and is ready for transplanting to another position.

ACHIEVING SUCCESS

One way of increasing the success rate with layering is to make a short slit in the underside of the stem at its lowest point. This checks the flow of the sap at this point and helps to promote rooting. Alternatively, a notch can be cut or some of the bark removed. Sometimes, just the act of forcing the stem down into a curve will wound the bark enough.

1 Make a shallow depression in the soil and place the selected stem in it. If the soil is in poor condition, remove some of it and replace it with potting compost (soil mix).

2 Use a metal pin or a piece of bent wire to hold the stem in place, if necessary, so that it cannot move in the wind.

3 Cover the stem with good soil or potting compost, and water it.

4 If you haven't pinned the stem down, place a stone on the soil above the stem, to hold it in position.

5 Once growth starts – or the stem feels as if it is firmly rooted when gently pulled – cut it away from the parent plant, ensuring that the cut is on the parent-plant side. Dig up the new plant and transfer it to a pot filled with potting compost. Alternatively, replant it elsewhere in the garden.

6 An alternative method is to insert the layer directly into a pot of compost, which is buried in the ground. Once the stem has rooted, sever it from the parent as above and dig up the whole pot. This is a good technique for making tip layers, as with this fruit-bearing tayberry. Tip layers are made by inserting the tip of a stem, rather than a central section, in the ground, until it roots; it is a suitable propagation technique for fruiting climbers, such as blackberries.

Right: *Roses are just one of the types of climber that can be propagated by layering.*

SHRUBS

Shrubs have a place in any garden and it is, in fact, impossible to imagine a garden without them. They provide so much: colour, shape, bulk, a habitat for wildlife, screens from the neighbours, dividers and even "camps" for children to play in. Flowering shrubs provide sudden bursts of colour. Some flower over a long period, but even those that do not are usually glorious while they last. In many cases, the visual power of the flowers is enhanced by a wonderful fragrance which wafts throughout the whole garden. There are flowering shrubs for every month of the year, including the depths of winter. Some can simply be enjoyed in the garden, while others may be cut to provide material for bunches of flowers for indoors or to give away.

Left: *This* Cotinus coggygria *'Royal Purple' is blessed with strikingly handsome, dark purplish-red leaves.*

DESIGNING A BORDER

Drawing a Border Plan

There are several ways of designing a border. The majority of gardeners undoubtedly go for the hit-and-miss approach, simply putting in plants as they acquire them. Then, if they feel inclined, they may move them around a bit to improve the scheme. Many good gardens have been created in this way but a more methodical approach tends to produce better results from the outset. However, do not be fooled: no method produces the best results first time. Gardening is always about adjustment, moving plants here and there to create a better picture or to change the emphasis or mood.

MAKING A SKETCH

The most methodical approach to designing a border is to draw up a plan and to work from this. Making a plan is one of the many enjoyable parts of gardening. It involves choosing the plants that you want to grow, sorting them into some form of pattern and committing this to paper, so that you can follow it through. A further refinement is to produce a drawing of what the border will roughly look like at different stages of the year. You do not have to be an artist to do this; it is for your own satisfaction and, since no one else need see it, the drawing can be quite crude!

The plan itself should, preferably, be drawn up on squared paper (graph). This will help considerably in plotting the size and relationship of plants. The sketches can be on any type of paper, including the back of an envelope, if you can't find anything else at the time.

Decide whether you are going to treat the garden as a whole or whether you are going to concentrate on a single border. This border will need to be accurately measured if it is already in existence or you must firmly decide on its intended shape and dimensions.

Draw up a list of the plants that you want to grow, jotting details alongside as to their colour, flowering period, eventual height and spread and their shape.

Plot the plants on the plan, making sure you show them in their final spread, not the size they are in their pots. Bear in mind details such as relative heights, foliage and flower colour. These can be further explored by making an elevation sketch of the border as seen from the front. It can be fun to colour this in with pencils or watercolours, to show roughly what it will look like in the different seasons.

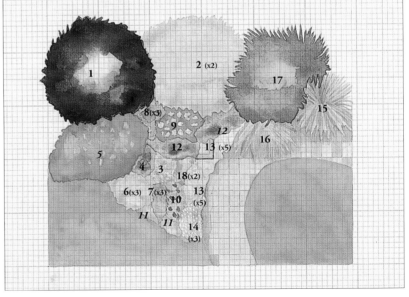

Key

1. *Cotinus coggyria* 'Royal Purple'
2. *Weigela florida* 'Florida Variegata'
3. *Perovskia atriplicifolia* 'Blue Spire'
4. *Allium chrisophii*
5. *Daphne x burkwoodii* 'Somerset'
6. *Sedum spectabile* 'September Glow'
7. *Eryngium giganteum*
8. *Digitalis purpurea*
9. *Rosa* 'Wenlock Castle'
10. *Papaver somniferum*
11. *Astrantia major*
12. *Salvia forsskaolii*
13. *Stachys byzantina*
14. *Lychnis coronaria* 'Alba'
15. *Yucca gloriosa* 'Variegata'
16. *Phormium cookianum*
17. *Berberis thunbergii* 'Rose Glow'
18. *Dictamnus albus purpureus*

Above: *It will take a few years before your plans and sketches develop into the established border you would like to see.*

Designing with Shrubs

Of all aspects of gardening, designing a garden or border is probably one of the most exciting and, at the same time, one of the most difficult. It requires the ability to see things that are not yet there and to assemble whole groups of different plants in the mind's eye.

THE BASIC ELEMENTS

Most people have an awareness of the basic elements of garden design from other disciplines; most of us, for example, are adept at choosing what clothes to wear. We know what colours go together and what suits our shape and height. We are aware that certain fabrics add a touch of luxury to an outfit and that certain colours create a bright effect, while others produce a more subtle image. Similarly, most people are at least involved in decorating their home, where again the choice of colours, textures and finishes have become almost second nature over the years.

PERSONAL TASTE

The same principles we apply to choosing clothes and items for the home are used when designing in the garden, with many of the choices coming from an innate feeling for what the gardener likes and dislikes. This means that, like clothing, gardens are personal, with the fortunate result that each garden is different from the next. By all means be inspired by ideas seen in other gardens, but do not slavishly imitate another garden: the chances are that it will not work in your situation – the climate might be slightly different or the soil might be wrong. There are no definite rules with regards to design; there is no ultimate garden. However, there are a few guidelines that the experience of many centuries of gardening have produced, and it is worth bearing these in mind.

THE SHAPE OF THE BORDER

A border can be any shape, to suit the garden. Curved edges tend to create a more informal, relaxed feeling, while straight edges are more formal. The one point to remember is that the border should not be too narrow. Shrubs look better in a border where they have room to spread without being too crowded. A border that is only wide enough to take one shrub at a time has a habit of looking more like a hedge than a border. A wider border also allows the gardener to build up a structure of planting, which is more visually satisfying.

Left: *An attractive border filled with a mixture of shrubs and herbaceous plants designed to provide interest over a long period of time. Shrubs in flower include the blue* Ceanothus, *white* Olearia, *purple* Lavandula stoechas *and the white* Prostanthera cuneata, *with a purple rhododendron in the background.*

PART OF THE SCHEME

Shrubs need not be confined to borders – they can become part of the overall scheme of the garden. This is particularly important where the garden is small and there is little room for formal borders. Shrubs can be mixed with other plants or simply used in isolation, as focal points that draw the eye. They can be taken out of the ground and used in pots or other containers, or grown against walls and fences. Besides being part of the design, they can have a sense of purpose, perhaps to screen a dustbin (trash can) or to create a perfumed area near where people sit in the evening.

HEIGHT AND SHAPE

Shrubs have a lot to offer the designer as there is such a wide choice of attributes that can be applied to them. Shrubs come in all sorts of shapes and sizes, from tiny dwarf ones to those that are difficult to distinguish from trees. The general principle of design is to put the tallest at the back and smallest at the front. This must not be rigidly adhered to or the the border will begin to look like choir stalls, all regularly tiered. Bring a few of the taller ones forward and place some of the shorter ones in gaps between bigger ones. This makes the border much more interesting and prevents the viewer from taking in the whole border at a glance.

The different shapes of the plants also add variety. Some are tall and thin, others short and spreading. The latter are particularly useful as ground cover and can be woven in and out of other shrubs as if they were "poured" there. Heathers are especially useful for this.

Above: *In this small garden, shrubs are not only used to make an interesting background of different textures, shapes and colours, but are also planted in containers to break up the foreground. To complete the picture, formal hedges hold the whole scheme together.*

Right: *This attractive border builds up beautifully from the front but, at the same time, is not regimented as the heights vary along its length. It demonstrates well the effectiveness of differently-shaped shrubs and other plants while, at the same time, illustrating the importance of colour and leaf shapes.*

Using Colour in the Border

Colour is an extremely important aspect of shrub gardening, perhaps more so than other areas because shrubs not only offer a large range of flower colours but also a vast range of foliage colour and texture.

MIXING COLOURS

Colour is the most tricky thing to get right in the garden. It is essential to spend time looking at other gardens and looking at pictures in books and magazines, to see how colours are best handled. It is not just a question of saying that reds mix well with purples: some do, others do not. Orange-reds and blue-reds are quite different from each other and cannot all be used in the same way.

A good garden will combine all the colours in a variety of ways in all areas. Sticking to just one style, especially in a large garden, can become boring. In a small garden, trying to mix too many different colour schemes has the reverse effect and may become uncomfortable.

Using shrubs gives colour in both leaves and flowers. When planning, it is important that the foliage of the various plants blends well together as they are generally around for a long time – all year, in fact, if they are evergreen. Try not to use too many different colours of foliage together and avoid too many variegated shrubs in one place as this can look too "busy". The colour of nearby flowering plants can also enhance the foliage.

Colours can also be affected by the texture of the leaves. A shiny green leaf can light up a dull area almost as brilliantly as a gold leaf while a soft, hairy foliage adds a sense of luxury.

Right: *The sharp contrast between the silver leaves of the* Elaeagnus *'Quicksilver' and the purple of the flowers of* Erysimum *'Bowles Mauve' makes a beautiful, if startling, combination.*

Below: *Here, the purple flowers of* Lavandula stoechas pedunculata *make a much softer contrast to the purple-leaved sage* Salvia officinalis *'Purpurascens'.*

Left: *The bright red stems of* Cornus alba *'Sibirica' add a great deal of interest to the winter scene, especially if sited so that the low sun strikes them.*

Right: *A dwarf willow,* Salix repens, *grows with the ground-hugging* Lithodora diffusa. *The contrast in the flowers makes this an exciting combination in the spring and, for the rest of the year, the different foliage shapes make them an interesting ground cover.*

COLOURFUL STEMS

It is not only the leaves and flowers of shrubs that have colour: stems, too, can provide it. This is particularly true in the winter, when the leaves are off most shrubs and there is little to lighten the grey scene. White, yellow, green, red and black stems then come into their own. Plants grown for their winter stems are often uninteresting for the rest of the year and so should be planted where they will not be noticed in summer but will stand out in winter.

Right: *It is possible to jazz up the appearance of the garden with bright colour combinations, such as this azalea and alyssum,* Aurinia saxatilis. *The dazzling picture they create is wonderful but, fortunately, neither plant lasts in flower too long, otherwise the effect would become tiresome.*

Mixing Shrubs

Shrub borders or shrubberies have died out as gardens have become smaller. In many ways, the border devoted to only shrubs would be a labour-saving form of gardening, but being able to mix in a few other plants helps to make it more interesting.

GROWING SHRUBS WITH PERENNIALS AND ANNUALS

As well as being more interesting from a visual point of view, mixing shrubs and other plants creates a greater variety of different habitats in the garden for a greater range of plants. For example, there are many herbaceous plants, many coming from wooded or hedgerow habitats in the wild, that need a shady position in which to grow. Where better than under shrubs? Many of these, such as the wood anemone, *Anemone nemorosa*, appear, flower and die back in early spring before the leaves appear on the shrubs, thus taking up a space that would be unavailable later in the season once the foliage has obscured the ground beneath the shrub.

Herbaceous plants can also be used to enliven a scene where all the shrubs have already finished flowering. For example, if you have a number of rhododendrons, most will have finished flowering by early summer and will be comparatively plain for the rest of the year. Plant a few herbaceous plants between them and retain interest for the rest of the year.

Herbaceous plants also extend the range of design possibilities. For example, it might not be possible to find a shrub of the right height that blooms at the right time with the right-coloured flowers. One of the thousands of hardy perennials may offer the perfect solution. Similarly, the combination of textures and shapes might not be available in shrubs, so look to see if there are herbaceous or annual plants that will help solve the problem.

In the early stages of the establishment of a shrub border or a mixed border, the shrubs are not likely to fill their allotted space. To make the border look attractive in the meantime, plant annuals or perennials in the gaps. These can be removed as the shrubs expand. As well as improving the appearance of the border, the plants will also act as a living mulch and help to keep weeds at bay.

WOODLAND PLANTS FOR GROWING UNDER SHRUBS

Anemone nemorosa (wood anemone)
Brunnera macrophylla
Campanula latifolia
Convallaria majalis (lily-of-the-valley)
Cyclamen hederifolium
Eranthis hyemalis
Euphorbia amygdaloides robbiae (wood spurge)
Galanthus (snowdrop)
Geranium
Helleborus (Christmas rose)
Polygonatum
Primula

Above: *This* Lychnis chalcedonica *adds the final touch to a good combination of foliage. Without it, the grouping might seem dull compared with other parts of the garden in the summer.*

Above: *The geranium in the foreground is the right height and colour to match the roses and the ceanothus behind. It would be hard to find a shrub to fit in with this combination.*

Left: *Sometimes, one startling combination acts as a focal point and draws the eye straight to it. This combination of the blue flowers of a ceanothus and the silver bark of the eucalyptus is extraordinarily beautiful. There are many such combinations that the gardener can seek and this is one of the things that makes gardening so satisfying and even, at times, exhilarating.*

Above: *A good combination of textures, shapes and colours is achieved here with the cardoon (*Cynara cardunculus*) providing interesting colour and structure, while the* Salvia sclarea *in the front provides the subtle flower colour.*

CHOOSING SHRUBS

Hedges

Few gardens are without a hedge of some sort. They are used as a defensive barrier around the garden as well as having a more decorative purpose within. The defensive role is to maintain privacy both from intruders and prying eyes (and, increasingly, against noise pollution). This type of hedge is thick and impenetrable, often armed with thorns to discourage animals and humans pushing through. Hedges also have less sinister functions, more directly related to gardening. One is the important role of acting as a windbreak to help protect plants. Another is to act as a foil for what is planted in front of it. Yew hedges, for example, act as a perfect backdrop to herbaceous and other types of border.

Above: *A formal beech hedge (*Fagus sylvatica*) makes a neat and tidy boundary to any garden. Beech, yew (*Taxus baccata*) and hornbeam (*Carpinus betulus*) also make good formal hedges as long as they are kept neat. They are all slow growing and need less attention than many others.*

USING HEDGES

Hedges are widely used within the garden, where they are perhaps better described as screens or frames. Screens are used to divide up the garden, hiding one area from view until you enter it. In some cases, the hedges are kept so low that they can hardly be called hedges; they are more like decorative edging to a border. Box reigns supreme for this kind of hedge. Others are informal hedges, in which the plants are allowed to grow in a less restricted way, unclipped, so they are able to flower, adding to their attraction. Roses and lavender are two popular plants for using like this.

We all want hedges that grow up as quickly as possible and usually end up buying one of the fastest growers. However, bear in mind that once grown to the intended height, these fast growers do not stop, they just keep growing at the same pace. This means that they need constant clipping to keep them under control. A slower growing hedge may take longer to mature, but once it does, its stately pace means that it needs far less attention. In spite of its slow-growing reputation, in properly prepared ground, yew will produce a good hedge, 1.5–2 m (5–6 ft) high in about 5 to 6 years from planting.

Right: *Although often much maligned, leyland cypress (x Cupressocyparis leylandii) makes a good hedge. The secret is to keep it under control and to clip it regularly. Here, although soon due a trim, it still looks attractive, as the new growth makes a swirling movement across the face of the hedge.*

Above: *This tapestry hedge is made up of alternate stripes of blue and gold conifers. Here, the bands have been kept distinct but, if deciduous shrubs are used, the edges often blend together, which gives a softer appearance.*

Above: *A country hedge makes an attractive screen around the garden. This one is a mixture of shrubs, all or most of them being native trees: there is box (Buxus sempervirens), hawthorn (Crataegus monogyna), hazel (Corylus avellana) and holly (Ilex aquifolium). The only problem with this type of hedge is that the growth rates are all different so it can become ragged looking, but then country hedges always are!*

Left: *An informal flowering hedge is formed by this firethorn (Pyracantha). The flowers make it an attractive feature while the powerful thorns give it a practical value as an impenetrable barrier. Flowering hedges should not be clipped as frequently as more formal varieties and trimming should be left until flowering is over.*

Above: *Informal hedges of lavender border a narrow path. The joy of such hedges is not only the sight of them but the fact that, as you brush along them, they give off the most delicious scent. Such hedges fit into a wide variety of different situations within a garden.*

Maintaining a Hedge

Planting a hedge in most respects is like planting any shrub. Prepare the ground thoroughly as the hedge is likely to stay in place for many years, possibly centuries.

INGREDIENTS FOR A HEALTHY HEDGE

Add plenty of organic material to the soil, both for feeding the hedge and for moisture retention. If the ground lies wet, either add drainage material or put in drains. Plant the hedge between autumn and early spring. For a thick hedge plant the shrubs in two parallel rows, staggering the plants in each. Water as soon as it is planted and keep the ground covered in mulch. Use a netting windbreak to protect the hedge if it is in an exposed position.

CLIPPING HEDGES

If a hedge is neglected, it soon loses a lot of its beauty. Regular trimming soon helps to restore this but it is also necessary for other reasons. If the hedge is left for too long, it may be difficult to bring it back to its original condition. Most can be restored eventually but this can take several years. A garden can be smartened up simply by cutting its hedges. Untrimmed hedges look ragged and untidy. Some types of hedging material need more frequent trimming than others, to keep them looking neat.

1 Cutting a hedge also includes clearing up the trimmings afterwards. One way of coping with this task is to lay down a cloth or plastic sheet under the area you are clipping and to move it along as you go.

2 When using shears, try to keep the blades flat against the plane of the hedge as this will give an even cut. If you jab the shears forward with a stabbing motion, the result is likely to be uneven.

WHEN TO CLIP HEDGES

Buxus (box)	late spring and late summer
Carpinus betulus (hornbeam)	mid/late summer
Chamaecyparis lawsoniana (Lawson's cypress)	late spring and late summer
*Crataegus (*hawthorn)	early summer and early autumn
x Cupressocyparis leylandii (leyland cypress)	late spring, midsummer or late spring, early autumn
Fagus sylvatica (beech)	mid/late summer
Ilex (holly)	late summer
Lavandula (lavender*)*	spring or early autumn
Ligustrum (privet)	late spring, midsummer and early autumn
Lonicera nitida (box-leaf honeysuckle)	late spring, midsummer and early autumn
Prunus laurocerasus (laurel)	mid-spring and late summer
Prunus lusitanica (Portuguese laurel)	mid-spring and late summer
Thuja plicata (thuja)	late spring and early autumn
Taxus (yew)	mid/late summer

3 A formal hedge looks best if it is given a regular cut. The top, in particular, should be completely flat. This can be best achieved by using poles at the ends or intervals along the hedges, with strings tautly stretched between them. These can be used as a guide. Take care not to cut the strings! If you have room to store it, make a template out of cardboard in the desired shape of the hedge so that the shape of the hedge is the same each time you cut it.

4 Keep the blades flat when you cut the top of a hedge. If it is a tall hedge, you will need to use steps rather than trying to reach up at an angle.

5 Power trimmers are much faster than hand shears and, in consequence, things can go wrong faster as well, so concentrate on what you are doing and have a rest if your arms feel tired. Wear adequate protective gear and take the appropriate precautions if you are using an electrically operated tool. Petrol- (gasolene-) driven clippers are more versatile, in that you are not limited by the length of the cord or by the charge of the battery, but they are much heavier than the electrically-powered equivalent.

6 Some conifers are relatively slow growing and only produce a few stray stems that can be cut off with secateurs (pruners) to neaten them. Secateurs should also be used for large-leaved shrubs, such as laurel (*Prunus laurocerasus*). This avoids leaves being cut in half by mechanical or hand shears, which always looks a bit of a mess.

Above: *A well-shaped hedge should be wider at the bottom than it is at the top. This allows the lower leaves to receive plenty of light and thus prevents the bottom branches from drying out.*

Ground Cover

One of the most valuable uses of shrubs is as ground cover. Ground cover is what its name implies, planting that covers the ground so that no bare earth shows. While there are obvious visual attractions in doing this, the main benefit is that ground cover prevents new weeds from germinating and therefore reduces the amount of maintenance required.

PLANTS FOR COVER

In the main, ground-covering plants are low-growing, but there is no reason why they should not be quite large as long as they do the job. Large rhododendron bushes form a perfect ground cover, for example, as nothing can grow under them.

Some ground-covering plants have flowers to enhance their appearance – heather (*Erica* and *Calluna*) and *Hypericum calycinum*, for example – while others depend on their attractive foliage – ivy (*Hedera*) and euonymus are examples.

Ground cover will not stop established weeds from coming through; it does inhibit the introduction of new weeds by creating a shade that is too dense for the seed to germinate and that starves any seedlings that do manage to appear.

SHRUBS SUITABLE FOR PLANTING AS GROUND COVER

Acaena
Arctostaphylos uva-ursi
Berberis
Calluna vulgaris (heather)
Cistus (rock rose)
Cotoneaster
Erica (heather)
Euonymus fortunei
Hebe pinguifolia 'Pagei'
Hedera (ivy)
Hypericum calycinum
Juniperus communis 'Prostrata'
Juniperus sabina tamariscifolia
Juniperus squamata 'Blue Carpet'
Lithodora diffusa
Pachysandra terminalis
Potentilla fruticosa
Salix repens
Stephandra incisa
Vinca minor (periwinkle)

Above: *A solid block of gold shimmers above the soil. The evergreen* Euonymus fortunei *'Emerald 'n' Gold' makes a perfect ground cover plant because it is colourful and dense.*

Right: *Prostrate conifers perform well. One plant can cover a large area and the texture and colour of the foliage makes it a welcome feature. They have the advantage of being evergreen and thus provide good cover all year round.*

Above: *The periwinkles, especially* Vinca minor, *make good ground cover. They are evergreen and will thrive in quite dense shade. However, if you want them to flower well it is better that they are planted more in the open.*

Above: *In the rock garden, the ground-hugging* Salix repens *rapidly covers a lot of territory. It can be a bit of a thug and needs to be cut back from time to time, to prevent it from spreading too far.*

Above: Lithodora diffusa *is one of those plants that straddles the divide between hardy perennials and shrubs, because it is classed as a subshrub. It provides a very dense ground cover for the rock garden and, in the early spring, makes a wonderful carpet of blue.*

Right: *By late summer and into autumn, much ground cover is looking a bit tired and jaded. However,* Ceratostigma plumbaginoides *is still flowering and presents a good choice of plant for providing colour at this time of year.*

Planting Ground Cover

The benefits of ground cover only occur if the ground has been thoroughly prepared. Any perennial weeds left in the soil when the shrubs are planted will soon come up through the cover as it will not control existing weeds, it will only prevent new ones germinating.

TENDING GROUND COVER

Once planted, the space between the shrubs should be constantly tended until the plants have grown together, and from then on they truly create ground cover. Take care when planning ground cover as it is not something you want to replant too often.

Although one of the aims of using ground cover is to reduce maintenance by cutting out weeding, it still requires some attention and may need trimming once a year. Ivy, for example, looks much better if it is sheared in the late winter or early spring and hypericum should be cut back after flowering.

1 It is important to remove any weeds from the soil where you are going to grow ground cover, otherwise the weeds will grow through the shrubs which will make them very difficult to eradicate.

2 Thoroughly prepare the soil in the same way as you would for any other type of shrub. Dig in plenty of well rotted organic material.

3 Position the plants in their pots so that you get the best possible layout, estimating how far each plant will spread. The aim is to cover all the bare earth eventually.

4 Dig holes and plant the shrubs. Firm them in so that there are no air pockets around the plants and then water the shrubs well.

5 The gaps between the plants may take a year or more to close up. In the meantime, plant annuals, perennials or other shrubs to act as temporary ground cover while the main plants spread. Arrange the "fillers" in their pots first, so you can create the most effective planting.

Right: *When you are satisfied with the arrangement you have, plant the fillers and water them in. Remove them when the main ground cover takes over.*

MAINTAINING GROUND COVER

1 Ground cover is often neglected and, because it is a low, permanent planting, it tends to collect all kinds of litter and rubbish. Take time to regularly clean through all your ground cover, removing any litter that is lurking between the leaves.

2 Most ground cover benefits from being trimmed back at least once a year. Here, the periwinkle *Vinca minor* is given a much-needed trim.

3 Regular trimming means that the ground cover grows at a more even rate, with fewer straggly stems. It looks tidier and healthier.

Dwarf Shrubs

In the small garden and the rock garden, dwarf shrubs are much more in keeping with the scale of things than large plants. Being small, they also have the advantage that you can grow more varieties in the same space.

USING DWARF SHRUBS

Size apart, dwarf shrubs are no different from the larger ones and are treated in exactly the same way. They can be used by themselves in rock gardens or separate beds. Or they can be mixed in with taller shrubs, perhaps in front of them or even under them. Many dwarf shrubs make very good ground cover plants. They can also be used in pots and other containers, either in groups or as specimen plants.

ROCK GARDEN SHRUBS

The really small dwarf shrubs are usually grown in the rock garden and even in troughs. Many are not much more than a few centimetres high. Like their larger brethren, they are equally grown for their foliage and flowers. Some are perfect miniatures of larger plants. *Juniperus communis* 'Compressa', for example, could be a large conifer seen through the reverse end of a telescope.

Above: *For those who like bright colours, nothing could fit the bill better than* Genista lydia. *In spring, it is absolutely covered with a mound of bright, gold-coloured, pea-like flowers. It looks good tumbling over rocks or a wall but can be used anywhere. It requires very little attention.*

Above: *Most ceanothus are large shrubs, often needing wall protection to bring them through the winter. C. 'Pin Cushion' is a miniature version for the rock garden. It still retains both the good foliage and the blue flowers that attract so many gardeners to this group of plants and has the advantage that it needs little attention.*

Above: *As well as the more common dwarf shrubs, there are many varieties that will appeal to those who may want to start a collection of unusual shrubs:* x Halimiocistus revolii *is one example. This beautiful plant spreads to form a mat of dark green leaves, dotted with white flowers in midsummer. It likes a well-drained soil but needs little attention.*

Above: *The rock rose* (Helianthemum) *is one of the great joys of dwarf shrubs. There are many different varieties, with a wide range of colours, some bright while others are more subtle. The colour of their foliage also varies, from silver to bright green. Rock roses are suitable for the rock garden, raised beds or mixed borders. They spread to make large sheets, but rarely get tall. They need to be sheared over after flowering, to prevent them from becoming too sprawling.*

Above: *There are a number of dwarf willows of which this,* Salix helvetica, *is one of the best. It forms a compact shrub with very good silver foliage. It can be used in a rock garden or wherever dwarf shrubs are required. It looks especially good with geraniums –* G. sanguineum, *for example – growing through it. This willow needs very little attention.*

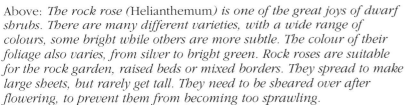

Left: *The group of dwarf conifers growing in this rock garden is* Juniperus communis *'Compressa'. This is one of the very best varieties of dwarf conifer, because it never grows very high, usually not more than 45 cm (18 in), and it takes many years to reach that height. Their slow growth rate means they are useful for alpine troughs and they have the advantage that they need very little attention.*

Above: *Using a few dwarf shrubs and conifers in a trough or sink adds to the height of the planting, giving it more structure and interest than if it were simply filled with low-growing alpine plants.*

Planting a Gravel Bed

Most dwarf rock garden plants need a well-drained soil with plenty of grit or sharp sand added to it. Plant between autumn and spring, as long as it is not too wet or cold. They look best grown with other alpine plants, set amongst rocks or in gravel beds. The miniature landscape of the trough can be designed in the same way.

1 Prepare the ground for planting. Dig the ground to allow about 5 cm (2 in) of gravel. Level the ground and lay heavy-duty black plastic or a mulching sheet over the area, overlapping strips by about 5 cm (2 in).

2 Tip the gravel on top of the plastic and level it off with a rake.

3 Draw the gravel back from the planting area and make a slit in the plastic. Plant in the normal way.

4 Firm in the plants and pull back the plastic, then cover again with gravel.

Right: *A rock garden with dwarf and slow-growing shrubs.*

DWARF SHRUBS FOR THE ROCK GARDEN

Aethionema
Berberis (dwarf forms)
Ceanothus prostratus
Chamaecyparis obtusa (and various 'Nana' forms)
Convolvulus cneorum
Convolvulus sabatius
Daphne
Dryas octopetala
Erica (heather)
Euonymus nana
Euryops acreus
Fuchsia procumbens
Genista lydia
x *Halimiocistus revolii*
Hebe (many dwarf forms)
Helianthemum (most forms)
Hypericum (many dwarf forms)
Juniperus communis 'Compressa'
Leptospermum scoparium 'Nanum'
Lithodora diffusa
Lonicera pyrenaica
Micromeria corsica
Ononis
Salix helvetica
Salix repens (and several other forms)
Sorbus reducta
Teucrium (various dwarf forms)
Thymus (many forms)
Verbascum 'Letitia'

WOODLAND BEDS

As well as a rock garden built in the sun, with free-draining material, many rock gardeners also have what is traditionally known as a woodland or peat bed, although other materials besides peat are now used for planting. The beds are positioned in part shade, where they catch dappled sunlight or sun only at the end of the day. Here, in a woodland-type soil, a wide range of plants that like damp, shady conditions can be grown. Amongst these are many dwarf shrubs, perhaps the most popular being the dwarf rhododendrons.

The soil here is usually a mixture of leaf mould and good garden soil. In the past, quantities of peat were also used, although a peat substitute, such as coir, is now commonly used instead. The soil is usually acidic in nature, suiting many of the plants that grow in woodland conditions. The peat, or peat substitute, gives it the right pH balance, although it is possible to make soil more acid by adding rotted pine needles to it.

DWARF SHRUBS FOR A WOODLAND BED

Andromeda
Arctostaphylos
Cassiope
Daphne
Erica (heather)
Gaultheria
Kalmia
Kalmiopsis
Pernyetta
Phyllodoce
Rhododendron (many dwarf forms)
Vaccinium

Above: *Daphnes are excellent dwarf shrubs to use in the garden. They all have deliciously scented flowers and many, such as this* D. tangutica, *are evergreen. They have the advantage that they very rarely need any pruning, just the removal of dead wood should any occur. They can be used in rock gardens or elsewhere.*

Top right: *Heathers make good all-year-round plants and appreciate the acid nature of a woodland bed.*

Right: *A colourful woodland bed can be made up of heathers and conifers. This kind of bed is low maintenance, although the heathers stay tighter and more compact if they are sheared over once a year.*

Evergreens

The great feature of evergreens is the fact that they hold on to their leaves throughout the winter. They can be used as a permanent part of the structure of any border or garden. This has advantages and disadvantages. The advantage is that throughout the year there is always something in leaf to look at; on the other hand, unless carefully sited, evergreens can become a bit dull, so plan your planting with care.

WORK-FREE GARDENING

In many respects, evergreen shrubs form the backbone of a work-free garden, because they need very little attention unless they are used as hedging, where they need regular clipping. Although they do not drop their leaves in autumn, as deciduous bushes do, they still nonetheless shed leaves. This is usually done continuously through the year.

Many evergreens have dark green leaves, which can make the scene in which they are used a bit sombre but this effect can be brightened with the use of plants with variegated leaves. Because evergreen leaves have to last a long time, many are tough and leathery, with a shiny surface. This shine also helps to brighten up dull spots, reflecting the light back towards the viewer.

Evergreens are no more difficult to grow than other shrubs; indeed they are easier because they need less maintenance.

Above: *Conifers can become boring and so familiar that you do not even see them. However, there are some that provide a wonderful selection of shapes and textures. This juniper produces an attractive "sea of waves" effect that can never become boring.*

Left: *Privet is a good evergreen shrub although in its common form it is better known as a hedging plant. This is* Ligustrum lucidum *'Excelsum Superbum'. In the open the variegation is golden but in shade it becomes a yellowish green.*

Left: *Choisya is a good evergreen. The leaves are shiny and catch the sun and it produces masses of white flowers in spring and often again later in the year. These perfume the air for a good distance around. This form with golden foliage is* C. ternata *'Sundance'.*

Above: *One tends to think of evergreens as being dull green and without flowers, but there are many that put on a magnificent display of flowers each year. Rhododendrons are a good example of this.*

Below: *This* Pieris japonica *is an evergreen that will grace any garden, as long as the area is not prone to late frosts. The foliage alters its colour as it matures, providing a constantly changing picture. This is enhanced by long plumes of white flowers.*

Above: *Many of the hebes are evergreen. This one,* H. cupressoides, *belongs to the whipcord group; it has very small leaves pressed tightly against its stems and, when out of flower, it could easily be mistaken for a conifer.*

Shrubs with Coloured Foliage

Most foliage is green, but the discerning gardener will soon notice that the number of different greens is almost infinite. A lot can be done by careful arrangement of these various greens, but even more can be achieved by incorporating into the garden the large number of shrubs that have foliage in other colours besides green.

VARYING SHADES OF GREEN

Leaves need green chlorophyll to function, so leaves are never completely devoid of green, another colour may just dominate. For example, yellow foliage still has a green tinge to it and purple likewise. Scrape back the hairs that make a leaf look silver or grey and, again, there will be green. When grown out of the sun, particularly later in the season, this green becomes more apparent. Occasionally, stems bearing paper-white leaves appear on some shrubs. It would be wonderful if one could propagate these by taking cuttings but, unfortunately, their total lack of chlorophyll means they will not grow.

MAINTAINING THE COLOUR

Purple leaves need the sun to retain their colour. Silver-leaved plants must always be grown in the sun; they will not survive for long in shade. Golden and yellow foliage often need a dappled shade – too much sun and the leaves are scorched. However, too much shade and the leaves turn greener, so the balance is a delicate one. The thing to avoid is midday sun.

Growing coloured-leaved shrubs is no different from any other shrub. They need the same pruning, except that if a reversion occurs, this must be cut out.

As well as shrubs with single-coloured foliage, there are shrubs with foliage in two or more colours, known as "variegated" foliage, and shrubs which are planted for their autumn foliage – just two other interesting aspects of the coloration of shrubs.

SILVER FOLIAGE

Caryopteris x clandonensis
Convolvulus cneorum
Elaeagnus 'Quicksilver'
Hebe pinguifolia 'Pagei'
Hippophaë rhamnoides
Lavandula angustifolia
Pyrus salicifolia 'Pendula'
Rosa glauca
Salix lanata
Santolina chamaecyparis
Santolina pinnata neapolitana

BETTER FOLIAGE

Coppicing or pollarding some coloured-leaved shrubs improves the quality of the leaves. It produces bigger and often richer-coloured foliage. Cut the plants back in the early spring, before growth begins. They will quickly regain their original size but the foliage will be bigger and better. *Sambucus* (elder), *Cotinus* (smoke tree) and *Rosa glauca* all benefit from this.

Above: Rosa glauca *has the most wonderful glaucous (grey- or blue-green) foliage with a purple-blue tint which contrasts well with the pink and white flowers. The foliage is improved by coppicing.*

POLLARDING

1 Cut back the stems to very short stubs, leaving perhaps one or two buds on each stem to grow. The treatment looks a bit drastic, but a mass of new shoots will be produced during the summer, with colourful stems in winter.

2 A head of brightly-coloured branches will stem from the base in the winter as on this *Salix alba vitellina* 'Britzensis'.

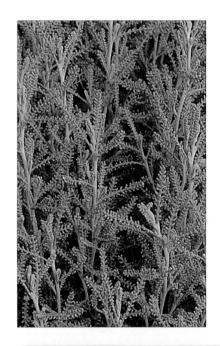

Left: *Silver foliage is very desirable. All silver plants need a sunny position and a well drained soil, this cotton lavender,* Santolina chamaecyparis *being no exception. Shear the plant over in the spring, just as new growth begins, to keep it compact. Many gardeners also prefer to cut off the flowering stems, because they find the sharp yellow flowers too harsh.*

Below: *This shrub grows in areas that are too dry to grow many other plants. It has had many names over the years and is now called* Brachyglottis *(Dunedin Group) 'Sunshine'.*

Above: *The silver leaves of plants can often set off the colour of their flowers beautifully. Here, the silvery-grey leaves of* Helianthemum *'Wisley Pink' are a perfect foil for its pink flowers. Shear over the plant after flowering, to keep it from becoming straggly.*

Above: *A favourite silver-leaved shrub is* Elaeagnus *'Quicksilver' which in the sunshine looks like burnished pewter. During the spring, the leaves are supplemented by masses of small, pale primrose-yellow flowers which as well as being attractive have a delicious scent that wafts all over the garden.*

Shrubs with Purple Foliage

Purple foliage is a very useful component when designing a garden. It forms a pleasant alternative to the normal green, without being quite as stark in contrast as silver, yellow or one of the variegated foliages.

A Pleasant Contrast

Purple is ideal as a main background colour or in combination with other plants as it goes with most other colours. It works well, in particular, as a background to various coloured flowers, so can be used with herbaceous or annual plants.

The one big drawback with purple foliage is that it can look very heavy and leaden if used in too great a quantity. A few shrubs will work better than too many. But purple can look superb if placed where the evening sunlight comes from behind the shrub so that the leaves are backlit. They then positively glow with colour and no other shrub can match them.

PURPLE-LEAVED SHRUBS

Acer palmatum
  'Atropurpureum'
Berberis thunbergii
  'Atropurpurea'
Berberis thunbergii
  'Bagatelle'
Cordyline australis
  'Atropurpurea'
Corylus maxima 'Purpurea'
Cotinus coggygria 'Royal
  Purple'
Fagus sylvatica 'Riversii'
Prunus cerasifera 'Nigra'
Salvia officinalis
  'Purpurascens'
Weigela florida 'Foliis
  Purpurea'

Above: *A really rich purple is to be seen on* Prunus x cistena. *This is beautifully enhanced in the spring by numerous pink flowers with purple centres. The total effect can be stunning.*

Left: *This* Cercis canadensis *'Forest Pansy' has purple foliage, exquisitely flushed with green and greenish blue. The heart-shaped leaves add to the attraction of this bush. In the autumn, the leaves take on a bright scarlet hue.*

Left: *The hazels (Corylus) have several purple forms to offer. They generally have large, imposing leaves. However, if they are in too shady a place they are liable to turn green.*

Right: *Another very good series of purples are the various smoke bushes,* Cotinus. *They look especially effective when they are planted so that the evening sun shines through the leaves. Cutting this shrub back hard in the spring produces much larger leaves the following year.*

Above: *In some shrubs, the colour is in the young leaves and once they begin to mature, they revert to their original colour. Although in some ways this is disappointing, in others, as here with this purple sage, the effect can be stunning.*

Above: *A good source of purple foliage is* Berberis thunbergii *'Atropurpurea' in its various forms, including a dwarf one. In the autumn, the leaves colour-up beautifully and the shrub has the added attraction of red berries.*

Shrubs with Variegated Foliage

There has been a steady increase of interest in variegated shrubs and today they can be seen in one form or another in most gardens. This increase of interest is most welcome, because it has stimulated the search for more types of variegated plants and now there are many more from which to choose.

TYPES OF VARIEGATION

There are many different types of variegation. First there is the aspect of colour. Most variegations in shrubs are gold, followed very closely by cream and white. These have the effect of lightening any group of plants they are planted with. They are particularly useful in shade or in a dark corner, because they shine out, creating interest where it is often difficult to do so. Other colours include different shades of green. Again, these have a lightening effect. On the other hand, variegation that involves purples often introduces a more sombre mood. Sometimes, there are more than two colours in a variegation and this leads to a sense of gaiety, even if combined with sombre colours.

When looked at closely there are several different patterns of variegation. From a distance the differences blur and the leaves just register as variegated, but if you get closer you can see how the variegation can alter the appearance of the leaves. In some cases, it is the edges of the leaves that are variegated, sometimes as a ribbon and in others as an irregular margin, perhaps penetrating almost to the centre of the leaves. Another common type is where the centre of the leaves are variegated. Sometimes this is an irregular patch in the centre and in others the variegation follows the veins of the leaf. Yet a third form of variegation is where the leaves are splashed with an alternative colour, as though paint has been flicked onto their surface. A final type is where the variegation appears as long parallel strips down the leaves.

All these are attractive and it is worth looking out for and collecting at least one of each type. The more one looks at this group of plants, the more fascinating they become.

SILVER AND WHITE VARIEGATION

Cornus alternifolia 'Argentea'
Cornus alba 'Elegantissima'
Cornus controversa 'Variegata'
Euonymus fortunei 'Emerald Gaiety'
Euonymus fortunei 'Silver Queen'
Euonymus fortunei 'Variegatus'
Euonymus japonicus 'Macrophyllus Albus'
Fuchsia magellanica 'Variegata'
Prunus lusitanica 'Variegata'
Rhamnus alaternus 'Argenteovariegata'
Vinca minor 'Argenteovariegata'

Above: *The variegated* Weigela florida *'Albomarginata' is seen here against a spiraea. The white-striped leaves blend well with the white flowers of the spiraea in spring, and in summer the interest is continued because the weigela produces pink flowers.*

Below: Cornus mas *'Aureoelegantissima' creates a very different effect here, by being planted next to a different type of plant. Here the colours are more muted and do not provide such a contrast as they do against the leaves of the* Geranium x oxonianum.

Above: *One of the most popular of variegated plants,* Cornus mas *'Aureoelegantissima', is shown here with* Geranium x oxonianum *growing through it. This is an easy plant to grow and its subtle coloration means it can grow in a wide variety of situations.*

Left: Rhamnus alaternus *'Argenteovariegata', as its name implies, has a silver variegation. This is present as stripes down the margins of the leaves and sets the whole shrub shimmering. It can grow into quite a large shrub, up to 3.5–4.5 m (12–15 ft) high.*

CUTTING OUT REVERSION IN SHRUBS

Variegation is an abnormality that comes about in a number of different ways. Frequently, the process is reversed and the variegated leaves revert to their original green form. These green-leaved stems are more vigorous than the variegated ones, because they contain more chlorophyll for photosynthesis and thus produce more food. If these vigorous shoots are left, they will soon dominate the shrub and it may eventually all revert to green. The way to prevent this is to cut out the shoots as soon as they are seen.

Above: *Green-leaved shoots have appeared in this* Spiraea japonica *'Goldflame'. If left, they may take over the whole plant. The remedy is simple. Remove the affected shoots back to that part of the stem or shoot where the reversion begins.*

Shrubs with Variegated Foliage 2

USING VARIEGATED PLANTS

Variegated plants should be used with discretion. They can become too "busy": if several are planted together they tend to clash. Reserve them to use as accent plants, to draw the eye. Also use them to leaven a scene, brightening it up a bit.

On the whole, variegated shrubs are no different in terms of planting and subsequent maintenance to any other plants, although you may need to consider how much sunlight they can tolerate.

Although many variegated shrubs will tolerate full sun, many others prefer to be away from the hot midday sun, in a light, dappled shade. Always check the planting instructions when you buy a new shrub, to see what situation it requires.

Above: *Several of the herbs, such as thyme, rosemary and sage, can be variegated. Here, the sage* Salvia officinalis *is shown in the yellow and green form 'Icterina'. As well as providing a visual attraction throughout the year, these evergreen variegated forms of herbs are also always available for use in the kitchen.*

Above: *This elder,* Sambucus racemosa *'Plumosa Aurea', is not, strictly speaking, a variegated plant, but the variation from the young brown growth to the golden mature leaves gives the overall impression of a variegated shrub. In order to keep this effect, prune the elder almost to the ground each spring.*

YELLOW AND GOLD VARIATIONS

Abutilon metapotamicum
 'Variegatum'
Aucuba japonica 'Picturata'
Aucuba japonica 'Mr Goldstrike'
Aucuba japonica 'Crotonifolia'
Caryopteris x clandonensis
 'Worcester Gold'
Cornus alba 'Spaethii'
Daphne x burkwoodii
 'Somerset Gold Edge'
Euonymus fortunei 'Sunshine'
Euonymus fortunei 'Gold Spot'
Euonymus japonicus
 'Aureopictus'
Ilex aquifolium 'Golden
 Milkboy' (centre)
Ilex aquifolium 'Aurifodina'
 (edge/centre)
Ilex x altaclerensis 'Golden
 King' (edge)
Ilex aquifolium 'Crispa
 Aureopicta' (centre)
Ilex x altaclerensis
 'Lawsoniana' (centre)
Ligustrum ovalifolium 'Aureum'
Osmanthus heterophyllus
 'Goshiki'
Sambucus nigra
 'Aureomarginata'

Above: *There are many variegated evergreens that can add a great deal of interest to what could otherwise be a collection of plain, dark green shrubs. The hollies, in particular, provide a good selection. This one is* Ilex x altaclerensis *'Lawsoniana'. Its green berries have yet to change to their winter colour of red.*

Above right: Berberis thunbergii *'Rose Glow' is a beautifully variegated shrub, its purple leaves splashed with pink. It is eye-catching and fits in well with purple schemes. Avoid using it with yellows.*

Right: *An exotic variegation is seen on this* Abutilon megapontamicum *'Variegatum', with its green leaves splashed with gold. It has the added attraction of red and yellow flowers that appear in the latter half of the summer and continue into the autumn. It is on the tender side and in colder areas should be grown in pots and moved inside for the winter.*

Shrubs with Fragrant Foliage

There are a surprising number of shrubs with fragrant foliage. Some fragrances might not be immediately apparent, because they need some stimulant to produce it. Rosemary, for example, does not fill the air with its perfume until it is touched. Some of the rock roses (*Cistus*) produce a wonderfully aromatic scent after they have been washed with rain. Similarly, the sweet-briar rose (*Rosa rubiginosa*) and its hybrids, such as 'Lady Penzance', produce a delightfully fresh scent after rain.

WHERE TO PLANT
It is a good idea to plant shrubs with aromatic foliage near where you walk, so that when you brush against them they give out a delicious aroma. Few gardeners can resist running their fingers through rosemary foliage as they pass, and a lavender path is a pleasure to walk along, because the soothing smells of the herb are gently released along the path as you go.

For hot, dry gardens, *Camphorosma monspeliaca* is one of the best plants to grow, because it smells of camphor when the new shoots are touched. Thyme planted in the ground may be too low to touch with the hands, but it releases its fine fragrance if it is walked on

in paving. Many conifers have a pleasant, resinous smell when they are rubbed. Juniper, in particular, is good.

But, of course, not all smells are pleasant. *Clerodendron bungei* has sweetly-scented flowers, but its leaves smell revolting if they are crushed. Many people dislike the sharp smell of the foliage of broom (*Cytisus*) and elder (*Sambucus*).

Above right: *While it is sensible to plant thyme used for the kitchen in a more hygienic position, it does make a wonderful herb for planting between paving stones because when crushed by the feet it produces a delicious fragrance – and trampling on it does not seem to harm the plant. Beware doing so in bare feet though, because there may well be bees on the thyme.*

Right: Prostanthera cuneata *is an evergreen shrub that has leaves with a curious aromatic scent that is very appealing. In spring, and again in the summer, white, scented flowers are produced, which look very attractive against the dark foliage.*

SHRUBS WITH FRAGRANT FOLIAGE

Aloysia triphylla
Laurus nobilis (bay)
Lavandula (lavender)
Myrica
Myrtus communis (myrtle)
Perovskia
Rosmarinus (rosemary)
Salvia officinalis (sage)
Santolina

Above: *One of the most beguiling of garden scents is that of rosemary, another culinary herb. If given a sunny well-drained site, this shrub will go on growing for many years, until its trunk is completely gnarled and ancient looking.*

Above: *Culinary herbs are a great source of scented foliage. Sage, for example, has a dry sort of herby smell, which will usually evoke in the passer-by thoughts of delicious stuffing mixtures. This is an evergreen and provides fragrance all year round.*

Right: Hebe cupressoides, *like so many plants, has a smell that is characteristically its own. It is a resinous type of fragrance that is reminiscent of the cypresses after which it is named.*

Shrubs with Fragrant Flowers

It is always worthwhile to include at least a few shrubs in the garden that have fragrant flowers. Unlike foliage scents, which generally need to be stimulated by touch, flower fragrances are usually produced unaided, and flowers will often fill the whole garden with their scent. This is particularly noticeable on a warm evening.

SOOTHING SCENTS

A good position for fragrant shrubs is next to a place where you sit and relax, especially after the day's work. The soft fragrance from the shrubs helps to soothe tiredness if put next to a seat or perhaps near an arbour or patio where you sit and eat. Psychologically, it can help to plant a shrub that has evening fragrance near the front gate or where you get out of the car, so that you are welcomed home by characteristically soothing scents. Choose an evening-scented shrub so that you do not get the scent on your way out in the morning, or you might not get to work at all! Another good position for a fragrant shrub is near a window or door that is often open, so the scents drift into the house.

As with foliage scents, some flowers smell unpleasant. Many dislike the smell of privet flowers, while the scent from *Cestrum parqui* is foetid in the day but sweet in the evening and at night.

One way to store summer fragrances is to turn some of the flowers into *potpourri*. Roses, in particular, are good for this.

In the winter, a surprising number of winter-flowering shrubs have very strong scents that attract insects from far away. Always try to include a few of these, such as the winter honeysuckles, in the garden.

FRAGRANT FLOWERS

Azara
Berberis x stenophylla
Clethra
Corylopsis
Daphne
Elaeagnus
Hamamelis (witch hazel)
Itea
Magnolia
Mahonia
Myrtus (myrtle)
Osmanthus
Philadelphus (mock orange)
Rhododendron luteum
Sarcococca (sweet box)
Skimmia

Above right: *Daphnes are a good genus of plants for fragrance, because they nearly all have a very strong, sweet scent.* Daphne x burkwoodii *is one of the largest of the genus, seen here in its variety 'Somerset'. When in full flower in the spring, it will perfume a large area.*

Right: *The Mexican orange-blossom,* Choisya ternata, *is another sweet-smelling shrub. It flowers in the spring and then sporadically again through the summer. The delightful flowers contrast with the glossy foliage.*

Above: *Not everybody likes the smell of elder flowers, and even fewer people like the smell of elder leaves, but the flowers do have a musky scent that is popular with many country people.*

Left: *Many flowers produce a sweet scent in the spring and early summer and this* Viburnum x juddii *and its close relatives are always amongst the best examples. It produces domes of pale pink flowers with a delicious perfume that spreads over quite a wide area.*

Above: Philadelphus *(mock orange) is one of the most popular of fragrant shrubs. The combination of the pure white flowers (sometimes tinged purple in the centre) and the sweet perfume seems to remind many people of purity and innocence. They flower after many of the other sweet-smelling flowers are over.*

Above: *The most popular perfumed shrub of all must surely be the rose. One of the advantages of many modern varieties of rose is that they continue to flower and produce their scent over a long period, often all the summer and well into the autumn. 'Zéphirine Drouhin' has a wonderful scent and is repeat-flowering. It can be grown either as a bush or as a climber and has the added advantage of being thornless.*

Shrubs with Berries and Fruit

It is not just the leaves and flowers that make a shrub worth growing. Flowering usually produces some form of seed, which is often carried in an attractive casing of fruit or berry. Two of the oldest fruiting shrubs to be appreciated, even back in ancient times, are the holly and the mistletoe.

Left: *Pyracantha makes a very decorative display of berries in the autumn. There are several varieties to choose from, with the berry colour varying from yellow, through orange to red. The berries are not only attractive but good food for the birds.*

THE APPEAL OF FRUIT

Fruit, either as berries, seed pods or even fluffy heads, often enhances the appearance of a shrub, especially if the fruit is brightly-coloured. Fruit bushes, such as gooseberries and red currants, can be fan-trained or grown as standards, and many berried shrubs have been specially bred to increase the range of colours. The firethorn (*Pyracantha*) can now be found with red, orange or yellow berries, for example.

Berries and fruit are not only attractive to gardeners, but to birds and other animals, so if you want to keep the berries buy a shrub like skimmia which will not be eaten by them.

One thing to bear in mind with berrying shrubs is that the male and female flowers may be on separate plants (skimmias and hollies, for example). Although they will both flower, only the female with bear fruit. So if you want fruit or berries, make sure you buy a male and a female.

Below: *It is important when buying pernettyas (Gaultheria mucronata) that you buy both a male and a female plant to ensure that pollination takes place. One male will suffice for several females that carry the berries.*

BERRIED SHRUBS

Chaenomeles (japonica)
Cotoneaster
Crataegus (hawthorn)
Daphne
Euonymus europaeus
Hippophaë rhamnoides
Ilex (holly)
Ligustrum
Rosa
Symphoricarpo
Viburnum opulus

Right: Piptanthus *is not totally hardy and is normally grown against a wall for protection. After its yellow flowers in spring, it produces these attractive pods, which decorate the plant in midsummer.*

Left: *When buying holly, ensure that you buy a berry-bearing form as not all carry them. Seen here in flower is* Ilex aquifolium *'Ferox Argentea'.*

Right: *Skimmias are good plants for the winter garden as they have very large, glossy berries, with the advantage that the birds do not like them, so they remain for a long period. Ensure you get a berrying form and buy a male to pollinate them.*

Below: *The cotoneasters produce a brilliant display of berries, as well as having attractive leaves and flowers. The berries are not too popular with birds and are often left until all the other berries have been eaten.*

Above: *Rose heps or hips provide an extension to the rose's season. The colour varies from variety to variety, with some being red and others orange, and some, such as* R. pimpinellifolia, *bearing black berries.*

Shrubs for Containers

Such is the versatility of shrubs that they can be grown successfully in containers as well as in the open ground. Container shrubs can be positioned on hard surfaces such as patios, walls or on steps. They can also be grown in roof gardens, on balconies or in basement plots.

WHY CHOOSE CONTAINERS?

If the garden is small or paved, there is no reason why all the plants should not be grown in containers, particularly because they can be attractive in their own right. Any kind of shrub can be grown in a container, so long as the shrub is not too big or the container too small.

One advantage of growing shrubs in pots is that you can tailor the soil to the shrub's requirements. Probably the best thing about this is the fact that it is possible to grow acid-loving plants, such as rhododendrons and azaleas, in areas where the soil is naturally alkaline and where such plants would not normally grow. Camellias, pieris, gaultherias, vacciniums and heathers are among other such plants which need special soil.

Above: *A glazed ceramic container is used to house a combination of lavender and* Euonymous fortunei *'Emerald Gaiety'; as long as they do not outgrow their container, such combinations can create a most attractive picture.*

Right: *Most elders make a large shrub after a few years, but they can still be used as pot plants, especially if cut to the base each spring. Here* Sambucus racemosa *'Plumosa Aurea' is growing in a large substitute-stone container. It is used as part of a larger planting.*

Above: *Fuchsias make exceptionally attractive container plants. The more tender varieties need to be over-wintered inside or started again each year, but hardier varieties can be left outside in milder climates.*

Above: *It is often possible to plant shrubs that form large bushes in containers for a few years while they are still small and then replace them with the same or another plant. Here Cornus mas 'Aureoelegantissima' which could eventually grow to 6 m (20 ft) or more is being used.*

Right: *Acid-loving shrubs like this rhododendron benefit from being grown in containers, where they can have the soil they need.*

SHRUBS FOR CONTAINERS

Ballota pseudodictamnus	*Ilex* (holly)
Buxus sempervirens (box)	*Indigofera*
Callistemon citrinus (bottlebrush)	*Kalmia*
Camellia	*Laurus nobilis* (bay)
Convolvulus cneorum	*Lavandula* (lavender)
Cordyline australis	*Myrtus communis* (myrtle)
Cotoneaster	*Olearia* (daisy bush)
Erica (heather)	*Phormium* (New Zealand flax)
Fuchsia	*Rhododendron*
Hebe	*Rosa*
Helianthemum	*Rosmarinus* (rosemary)
Hydrangea	*Skimmia*
Hypericum	*Yucca*

Planting Shrubs in Containers

There is no great difficulty in growing plants in containers, so long as you remember that the pots are likely to need watering every day, except when it rains, and possibly more often than this in the summer.

CONTAINER CARE

When planting shrubs in containers, it is essential to use a good potting compost (potting soil) that contains plenty of grit or sharp sand, to help with drainage, and to add small stones to the pot so that excess water can drain away. In addition, a slow-release fertilizer and some water-retaining granules will encourage the plant to flourish.

Bear in mind that your plant will not grow indefinitely if it is kept in the same pot or compost (soil mix) for ever. Every year or so, remove the shrub and repot it using fresh compost. If the shrub is becoming pot-bound, that is, the roots are going round the edge of the container, forming a tight knot, either put it in a larger pot or trim back some of the offending roots.

POSITIONING CONTAINERS

If you have a large enough garden, it is possible to keep the containers out of sight and only bring them into view when the shrubs are at their best, in full flower, for example. In a smaller garden, where this is more difficult, move the pots around so that the best ones are always in the most prominent position and even hiding the others if this is possible.

1 All containers should have a drainage hole in the bottom. Loosely cover this and the bottom of the pot with broken pottery, bits of tile or small stones, so that any excess water can freely drain away.

2 Partially fill the container with compost (soil mix) and then mix in some water-retaining granules. These essential granules will swell up and hold many times their own weight in water to give up to the plant's roots when they want it. While not considerably reducing the amount of water needed, water-retaining granules will make it easier for the shrub to come through really hot and dry times in midsummer. Follow the instructions on the packet as to quantities you need for the size of the pot you have.

3 Place the container in the position you finally want to have it and continue filling it with compost (the pot will be heavy to move once it is fully-planted). Plant the shrub to the same level as it was in its original container. Firm the compost down lightly and top up, if necessary, with some further compost.

4 Most composts contain fertilizers but the constant watering will soon leach (wash) it out. A slow-release fertilizer can be mixed with the compost or a tablet, as here, can be added to the pot, which will give six months' supply of nutrients. Read the packet for any special instructions.

5 Leave the top of the compost as it is, or cover it with stones of some sort, such as large pebbles, as here, or gravel. These not only give the container an attractive finish but help keep the compost cool and prevent water from evaporating.

6 Finally, water the container thoroughly and continue to do so at regular intervals. During hot weather, this is likely to be at least daily.

7 You may want to keep the newly-planted pot out of sight until the shrub has matured or comes into flower. However, if the container is large, it is often best to fill it *in situ*, because it will be very heavy once filled with compost.

Right: *This variegated pieris, which likes an acid soil, would soon languish and die in a chalky garden.*

Shrubs for Topiary

Most shrubs are grown naturally. They may be cut back if they get too big, or trimmed if they are part of a hedge, but their natural shape is not generally altered. However, there is one class of shrub-growing in which the shape is drastically altered, so much so that it takes a close look to identify the plants involved. These are topiaries.

PRODUCING A SHAPE

Topiaries can be cut to any shape the gardener desires. They can be formed into abstract or geometrical shapes, such as balls, cones or pyramids, or they can be made into something more intricate, perhaps depicting a bird, a person or even a teapot. There is little limit to what the imagination can produce in topiary.

Tight, slow-growing shrubs are the ones to choose for topiary, with yew and box being the best. Holly (*Ilex*), privet (*Ligustrum*) and box-leaf honeysuckle (*Lonicera nitida*) are also recommended. Several others can also be used, but they need a lot more attention to keep them neat.

The simplest topiaries are "carved" out of solid shrubs, particularly if they are yew or box, because these will easily regenerate and slowly fill out to their new shape. However, the most satisfactory way to produce topiary is to train the shrubs to their shape from the very beginning. A metal or wooden former or template helps with this. The shoots are tied in and trimmed as they grow, until the shrub has acquired the desired shape. Some formers are just a rough guide to the shape, intended to hold the main pieces in position, especially if they are

vulnerable, such as a peacock's tail, but others are shaped like the finished work and can be used as a trimming guide when the work is complete.

Topiaries can take several years to reach completion, so do not get too impatient. Several projects can be started in pots at the same time, so there is always something going on to keep the interest alive.

TOOLS FOR TOPIARY

Unless the topiary is on a large scale, avoid using powered tools. It is too easy to lose concentration or momentary control and disaster follows. In preference, use hand tools, which take longer but which give you more control. For cutting thicker stems, especially in the initial training, use secateurs (pruners), snipping out one stem at a time. Once the shape has been formed, trim it over with normal hedging shears or a pair of clippers of the type usually used for sheep-shearing. The latter give excellent control, but can only be used for light trimming, such as removing the tips of new growth. If the topiary is made from a shrub with large leaves, then use secateurs to trim it to avoid cutting the leaves in half, otherwise they will die back with a brown edge and the overall appearance will be spoiled.

Above: *In this topiary a four-masted ship in full sail glides across the garden. Here, the complicated design is slightly obscured by other topiaries in the background.*

Above: *This practical piece of topiary has a wooden seat worked into the bottom of the shrub, supported on a metal frame. A complete set round a table would be a novel feature for a barbecue or outdoor meal.*

Above: *These simple shapes worked in box can be used to advantage in a wide variety of positions in the garden. They will take several years of dedication to produce, but the effort is definitely worth it.*

Above: *Gardens do not have always to be serious: there is a sense of fun about this jolly witch, sitting around her cauldron with her cat and its mouse, which would cheer up anybody looking at it.*

Above: *Topiary shapes can be as precise or as free as you wish. In this free interpretation of a simple windmill, cut from yew, you can sense the pleasure of the person who created it.*

SHRUBS FOR ALL SEASONS

Shrubs in Spring

Shrubs come into their own in the spring. This is the time when everything is waking up and looking fresh and the gardener's own enthusiasm is at its greatest.

SPRING FLOWERS

Many shrubs flower in spring, which gives them ample time to produce seed and for it to ripen and be distributed to ensure the next generation.

The one big enemy of spring-flowering shrubs is the severe late frosts that occur in some areas. A false start to the spring brings warm weather and then a sudden frost kills all the new shoots and knocks off the flower buds. Rhododendrons, azaleas, pieris, magnolias and many others frequently suffer this fate. One solution is to give some protection if hard frost is forecast. Placing a sheet of fleece over them is often sufficient.

It is tempting to put all the spring shrubs together, for one glorious display, but resist this or, at least, mix in a few later-flowering ones as well or the area could become dull for the rest of the year. One solution is to plant *viticella* clematis through them. These are cut back to the ground in late winter so that they do not interfere with the shrubs' flowering, but grow up and cover them in blooms from midsummer onwards.

Try and finish planting any new shrubs by early spring and, as the various shrubs finish flowering, prune them as necessary. Remember to feed those that are in containers.

Above: *The flowering currant,* Ribes sanguineum, *is a beautiful spring-flowering shrub, but its foliage has a distinctive 'foxy' smell that not everyone likes.*

Above: *Camellias flower from the late winter through to the middle of spring. They are best planted where they do not get the early-morning sun, as this will destroy the buds if they have been frosted overnight.*

Right: *One of the earliest shrubs to flower is* Spiraea 'Arguta' *which produces a frothy mountain of pure white flowers over quite a long period. Sometimes it will even produce a few blooms in midwinter, to brighten the gloom.*

Above: Exochorda x macrantha *'The Bride' is a showy, spring-flowering plant. When in full flower, it is so covered in pure white flowers that the leaves are barely visible. Here, many of the flowers are still in bud, forming attractive ribbons of white balls.*

Above: *Rhododendrons are many gardeners' favourite spring shrub. They need an acid soil and a position out of hot sunlight. They can be bought in a wide variety of colours, some soft and subtle and others bright and brash.*

Above: *Forsythia creates one of the biggest splashes of colour in the spring. Here it is used as an informal hedge. It should be cut immediately after flowering to ensure that new flowering shoots grow in time for next season.*

Right: *One of the best-loved spring shrubs is* Magnolia stellata. *Each year it is a mass of delicate star-like flowers in glistening white or tinged with pink. The effect is enhanced because the flowers appear on naked stems, before the leaves develop.*

Left: *Azaleas are a form of rhododendron. There are evergreen and deciduous forms, both producing masses of flowers in a good year. Many of the deciduous forms have a wonderful scent. Like other rhododendrons, they need an acid soil and shelter from hot sun.*

Left: *Berberis are versatile plants, because they are attractive for much of the year: they have spectacular flower displays in spring and good foliage until summer, which then becomes beautifully tinted in the autumn. As an extra, many varieties produce red berries, which often last throughout the winter. Shown here is* Berberis linearifolia *'Orange King'.*

Left: *Lilac* (Syringa) *flowers in the late spring. It has one of the most distinctive smells of all spring-flowering shrubs and is popular for cutting to take indoors. When the flowers die they can look ugly, especially the white forms, and should be removed.*

Above: *A close up of a berberis in flower. This one is* Berberis *'Goldilocks'. Many varieties have sweetly-scented flowers, and all are much loved by bees.*

SPRING-FLOWERING SHRUBS

Berberis	*Magnolia*
Camellia	*Mahonia*
Chaenomeles (japonica)	*Pieris*
	Prunus (cherry)
Corylopsis	*Rhododendron*
Corylus (hazel)	*Ribes* (currant)
Cytisus (broom)	*Rosmarinus* (rosemary)
Daphne	*Salix* (willow)
Exochorda	*Spiraea*
Forsythia	*Viburnum*

Shrubs in Summer

While spring is noted for its fresh, young flowers, summer, especially early summer, is the time of mainstream flowering. This is the time for heady scents, particularly on long, warm, summer evenings. It is also a time when insects are at their busiest, with flowering shrubs full of bees and butterflies. Buddleja, in particular, is good for both.

ENJOYING THE SUMMER

Mix in a few summer-flowering shrubs with those from earlier in the year, so that the garden or borders have some form of continuity. Plant fragrant shrubs near where you sit or relax, and use those with thick foliage to create areas of privacy.

There are many types of shrub or dwarf tree that can be used for producing fruit. Currants, gooseberries, cherries, plums and apples can all be grown as small shrubs. These have decorative blossoms in the spring and then provide the delights of picking your own fruit in the summer and autumn. They need not be in a special fruit garden; grow them in ordinary borders, but beware that the soft fruits may need netting, as they ripen, to prevent birds from eating them.

In a small garden, use large shrubs, rather than trees, to create a shady sitting area. There are many that can be used and they are better suited to being cut to shape than trees.

Generally, there is not much to be done to shrubs during the summer. If the garden is in a town or near a road where there is a lot of dust and grime, wash off the leaves with a sprinkler, or spray if there is a prolonged period of drought, because the film over the surface of the foliage will impair the shrub's ability to make food. Also water, if necessary. Continue to feed those shrubs in containers until the end of the summer.

Above: *In summer the bush* Olearia x haastii *resembles a snowy mountain. Shown in full flower, this one is delicately fronted by a variegated grass,* Phalaris arundinacea *'Picta', more commonly known as "gardener's garters". Always consider the relationship between plants, rather than simply putting them in at random.*

Left: *Roses are at their best in summer. Some are once-flowering and do so in the early summer, but many go on flowering throughout the whole summer. Some gardeners prefer to have a separate garden or special beds for roses, while others like to mix them in with other plants. This lovely old rose is* R. *'Stanwell Perpetual'.*

Above: *From midsummer onwards, the hydrangeas begin to flower. There is a wide range available. The delicate lace-caps are popular because of the shape of the flowers. Here, the beautiful* H. quercifolia, *or oak-leafed hydrangea, combines good flowers and good foliage. Another very attractive hydrangea to consider is* H. aspera *'Villosa', which has soft, furry leaves and subtle, mauvish-blue and pink flowers.*

Above: *Many hydrangeas have white flowers. On the whole, they prefer a shady position and here the whites come into their own, illuminating their surroundings.*

Left: *The vexed question with these mop-headed (*H. macrophylla*) varieties of hydrangea is the colour. The same plant can have blue flowers on acid soil, red ones on a neutral soil and pink ones on an alkaline soil. It is possible to vary the colour by changing the acidity of your soil but, in the long run, it is more satisfactory to go with what you have. If you want to have different colours, plant hydrangeas in containers with the appropriate soil.*

Left: *The rock roses, or* Cistus, *make very fine summer-flowering plants. They are especially good in hot summers as they need a dry soil and can happily cope with droughts. The flowers only last a day, but are replaced by fresh ones the following morning. Some species drop their petals in the early afternoon so they are not much use to the evening gardener. This one is* C. x skanbergii, *with white-centred pink flowers set off against soft, greyish-green foliage.*

Below: *The kalmias are not seen so frequently as they should be. This may be because they need an acid soil and light shade, but even gardeners with alkaline soils should be able to grow them in containers. They flower in early summer, covering the branches with pink or red flowers. These are held in bunches, each flower being cup-shaped in a way that is unique to the plant.*

Above: *Allied to the rock rose, and liking the same kind of hot, dry conditions, are the halimiums. These are evergreen, with white or yellow flowers, some varieties having brown blotches at the base of the petals. This one is* Halimium x pauanum, *a form with pure golden flowers. Again, the flowers are produced afresh each day over a long period through the summer and sometimes well into autumn.*

Above: *The lavateras have become popular with gardeners, and justifiably so. They produce flowers over a long period, from early summer right through to the first frost. Sometimes, after a severe winter, the stems are cut to the ground and, because the new shoots take a time to grow, the flowering does not start until much later in the summer. They are not long-lived plants and it is wise to take cuttings regularly, which is not a difficult task as they root easily.*

Above: *Californian lilacs, Ceanothus, are good-value plants. Although a few of them are deciduous, the majority in cultivation have evergreen foliage that stays attractive throughout the year. In the early summer, they are covered with masses of blue flowers, the shade of blue varying from light to dark, depending on the variety. This is the dwarf form, 'Pin Cushion'.*

Above: *Being closely related, the halimiums and the cistus produce crossbreeds of which this* x Halimiocistus revolii *is an example. The first part of the name is a combination of those of its parents. This shrub makes a low-spreading carpet of green foliage, which contrasts well with its myriad snow-white flowers.*

Above: *The New Zealand tea tree,* Leptospermum *is becoming increasingly popular, especially in milder areas. They flower over a long period, with masses of small, saucer-shaped flowers in red, pink or white, often with a dark centre. There are also double-flowered varieties and several dwarf forms that are good for rock gardens. This one is* L. scoparium *'Lyndon'.*

Above: *The New Zealand hebes are amongst some of the best summer-flowering plants. They make beautifully-shaped shrubs, with good foliage and masses of flowers that are produced over a long period. The long spikes of flowers seem to whizz around in all directions, like fireworks.*

SUMMER-FLOWERING SHRUBS

Abutilon	*Hydrangea*
Brachyglottis	*Hypericum*
Buddleja	*Indigofera*
Callistemon (bottlebrush)	*Jasminum*
Carpenteria	*Kalmia*
Ceanothus (Californian lilac)	*Lavandula* (lavender)
Cistus (rock rose)	*Lavatera*
Cornus (dog wood)	*Leptospermum*
Deutzia	*Leycesteria*
Erica (heather)	*Olearia* (daisy bush)
Fremontodendron	*Philadelphus* (mock orange)
Fuchsia	*Potentilla*
Halimium	*Rosa*
Hebe	*Sambucus* (elder)
Hibiscus	*Viburnum*
Hoheria	*Weigela*

Above: *Another plant from the same region as the New Zealand hebes is the Australian bottlebrush,* Callistemon. *This shrub has curious bottle-shaped flowers, that explain its common name. Being of Australian origin, they are on the tender side, but some can be brought through to survive most winters by planting against a warm wall. If in doubt, plant in a container and keep inside during the cold months. This species is* C. sieberi.

Right: *Various forms of* Abutilon vitifolium *are appearing in more and more gardens, because it is realized that they are frost hardy. They will not survive a severe winter, but they are quick-growing and can easily be replaced. They come in a range of colours, including red, white and mauve, as here.*

Shrubs in Autumn

Autumn sees the closing of the annual growing cycle. With it come the autumn tints and hues both of the foliage and of the many berries and other fruits. Autumn is the season of reds and browns.

LONG-FLOWERING SHRUBS

There are not many shrubs that flower just in the autumn, but some summer ones continue right through to the frosts. Fuchsias are particularly useful. Buddlejas, hibiscus, hydrangeas, hypericums and indigoferas also continue to flower. One of the true autumn-flowering plants is *Osmanthus heterophyllus*, with its fragrant flowers more reminiscent of spring than of summer. Other plants that are associated with autumn flowering are the ceratostigmas and Eucryphia glutinosa.

AUTUMN LEAVES

The true glory of the autumn belongs to foliage. In a small garden, in particular, it is a wise choice to make every plant earn its keep, and those that provide a fiery end to the year's gardening certainly deserve their place. Berries and other fruit are an added bonus; they are not only attractive but also supply birds and other animals with food for the harsh months ahead.

Autumn is the time to start preparing beds for new planting and indeed to actually start planting. It is also a time to check that those plants that need staking are still securely held in place, before the winter winds begin. Once the leaves have fallen, it is a good idea to go round and examine each shrub, removing any dead or dying wood. Autumn is also the time for clearing up fallen leaves and stopping them from smothering other plants and lawns. Do not waste them by burning or throwing them away. Compost them and return them to the soil once they have rotted.

Right: *While the best-known Osmanthus flower in the spring,* O. heterophyllus *flowers in late autumn, perfuming the air.*

Below: *Hydrangeas are really summer-flowering shrubs, but their flowers last such a long time that they are still flourishing well into autumn, when their leaves lose their green colour and take on autumn tints.*

SHRUBS WITH GOOD AUTUMN FOLIAGE

Amelanchier
Berberis thunbergii
Ceratostigma willmottianum
  (leaves and flowers)
Cotinus (smoke bush)
Enkianthus
Euonymus alatus
Fothergilla
Rhus hirta
Stephandra incisa

SHRUBS WITH GOOD AUTUMN FLOWERS

Buddleja
Ceratostigma
Eucryphia glutinosa
Fuchsia
Hibiscus
Hydrangea
Hypericum
Indigofera
Osmanthus heterophyllus

Above: *The Judas tree is a curious shrub. In spring, purple flowers fill the naked branches; in autumn the leaves take on beautiful colours.*

Left: *Some of the most brilliant of autumn colours are presented by the spindle trees and bushes,* Euonymus. *The colourful* E. alatus *'Compactus' is suitable for the smaller garden. Interest in winter is maintained by its corky wings on the stems.*

Above: *Berberises provide the gardener with a valuable group of plants. They are attractive at all seasons of the year, providing flower, berry and foliage interest. Most produce fiery-coloured foliage and waxy red berries in the autumn, including this* B. thunbergii *'Red Pillar.'*

Above: *Blue is not a colour that one normally associates with the autumn; indeed there are not many shrubs that produce flowers of this colour at any time of year.* Ceratostigma willmottianum *has piercingly blue flowers that carry over from summer well into autumn.*

Right: *Most of the* eucryphias *soon become large trees, but* E. glutinosa, *although it can become large, usually remains small enough to be considered a shrub. The beauty of this plant is the late-season flowers. They are glisteningly white bowls, with a central boss of stamens.*

Left: *As well as its beautiful flowers,* Eucryphia glutinosa *is deciduous, and its leaves take on autumnal tints.*

Above: *Fothergill (*Fothergilla major*) is another good-value shrub with good flowers in late spring or early summer and wonderfully-coloured foliage in autumn. It is very slow growing and although it can eventually become quite large, it will take many years to do so.*

Below: *Many of the cotinus, or smoke bushes, have foliage that is attractive throughout the growing seasons. Many are dark purple, which beautifully set off their smoky plumes of flowers.*

Above: Amelanchier lamarckii *frequently grows into a small tree but, if required, it can be pruned to produce several stems instead of a trunk, so that it becomes a large shrub. It is covered with delicate white flowers in spring and then in autumn its leaves colour beautifully.*

Shrubs in Winter

Winter is often considered the dead month in the garden and many may be tempted to stay indoors. But, in fact, there is a lot going on. A number of shrubs flower at this time of year, some of them with beautiful scents that are particularly noticeable on warm winter days. There are also evergreen shrubs that can look particularly good in the low winter light, especially those with shiny leaves.

WINTER TASKS

There is a lot going on during the winter months and the garden should reflect this. Because many of the shrubs that provide winter interest are dull at other times, they should be planted in less prominent positions. In this way, they will show up in winter when other plants have died back, but will be masked by more interesting plants for the rest of the year.

If the weather is fine and the soil not waterlogged, work can proceed. The more achieved during these winter months, the less there will be to do later in the year. If all the beds are forked over, the weeds removed and the soil mulched, the need for weeding throughout the spring and summer will be considerably reduced. Indeed, one hour spent weeding in winter will save several later on. Provided that the ground is neither waterlogged nor frozen, this is also the best time of year for planting and moving shrubs.

During snowy weather, make certain that shrubs, especially evergreen ones, are not weighed down and broken by excessive falls. Knock the snow off at the earliest opportunity. Light falls should be left if there is a cold wind, because these will help protect the plants.

Above left: *The winter jasmine,* Jasminum nudiflorum, *is truly a winter plant, flowering from the end of autumn through into the early spring, totally ignoring the frost and snow. Stems taken indoors make attractive winter flower decorations.*

Above right: *The winter hazels,* Corylopsis, *make excellent winter plants, with yellow catkins that defy the frosts.*

Right: *Witch hazels,* Hamamelis, *produce curious flowers like clusters of ribbons. As well as being attractive, they have a strident smell that fills the air on sunny days.*

SHRUBS WITH WINTER INTEREST

Corylus (hazel)
Cornus mas (dog wood)
Corylopsis
Hamamelis (witch hazel)
Jasminum nudiflorum
Lonicera purpusii
Lonicera standishii
Lonicera fragrantissima
Mahonia
Viburnum bodnantense
Viburnum farreri
Viburnum tinus

Above and below: *Like many winter-flowering shrubs, the mahonias are beautifully scented. This is possibly to make certain that they attract what few insect pollinators there are at this time of year. Mahonia is a prickly subject and plants can look a bit tatty at some times of year, but in winter it is supreme, with its long spikes of yellow flowers and wafting scent.*

Left: *Viburnums are a versatile group of plants, with at least one variety in flower at each time of year, including two or three in winter. Viburnum tinus is evergreen and is covered with flat heads of flowers throughout most of the winter and often through to the spring as well. On warm days the flowers have a delicate perfume.*

Shrubs with Coloured Stems

Those shrubs that have coloured bark and are grown for their winter stems such as *Rubus cockburnianus, R. thibetanus* and *Salix alba* 'Britzensis' are very worthwhile and are of great value to the winter gardener.

WINTER STEMS

When the leaves have fallen from the shrubs it is time to appreciate what is left: the bare outline of the stems and branches and, more importantly, the colour of the bark. Not all shrubs are coloured in this way but a number provide a wonderful display, especially if they are planted so they catch the low winter sunshine. The shrubs are best cut to the ground each spring, so that there is new growth for the following winter.

SHRUBS WITH COLOURED WINTER STEMS

Cornus alba
Corylus avellana contorta
Rubus cockburnianus
Rubus thibetanus
Salix alba 'Britzensis'

Above: *The red glow of the stems of* Cornus alba *is seen here on a typical winter's day.*

Above: *The ghostly stems of* Rubus cockburnianum *shine out in the winter landscape. The white is a "powdery" bloom, which is lost on older stems, and the whole plant should be cut to the ground each spring to produce new stems for the following winter.*

Above: Cornus stolonifera *'Flaviramea' is quite vibrant with its yellowish green bark. If left to mature, the stems lose their rich colour and hard pruning every spring will ensure plenty of new growth for the following winter.*

Above: Rubus *'Golden Veil'* *is an extremely attractive plant, with bright yellow foliage in the summer and white stems in the winter. Here the leaves have nearly all fallen, revealing the attractive winter stems beneath.*

Right: *Several of the willows have beautiful winter stems as well as providing their distinctive catkins or pussies at the end of the season.* Salix alba *produces some of the best coloured stems. Here it is represented by* S.a. vitellina *and its variety* S.a.v. *'Britzensis'. The stems should be cut back each spring to encourage new growth for the following winter.*

Left: *Here* Salix gracilistyla *'Melanostachys' displays the catkins typical of so many willows in the winter. As well as being attractive in the garden, the stems are very popular for adding to indoor winter flower arrangements.*

CLIMBERS

Climbers do not seem to have any shape: they just go straight up – or do they? When you stop to think about it you realize they are actually much more versatile. For a start, they can be trained to spread sideways, thus covering a considerable area, or even grown through trees and shrubs. Climbers are slightly more difficult to grow than shrubs, simply because they need something to climb up and usually an element of training. However, the choice of training method gives the gardener plenty of scope. Climbers can be grown on walls with a variety of supports, including wires and trellis panels. Trellising can also be used to form fences or screens, either around the outside of the garden or within it. Archways, arbours and pergolas are other ideal supports for climbers.

Left: *Golden hop* (Humulus lupulus *'Aureus') is an attractive, self-supporting perennial climber with bristly twining stems.*

TYPES OF CLIMBERS

Annual Climbers

When considering climbers, most gardeners automatically think of woody climbing plants, such as clematis or roses, and forget about the annuals. However, annual climbers are extremely useful plants and should never be overlooked.

INSTANT COLOUR

One of the great virtues of annual climbers is that they are temporary; they allow the gardener the opportunity of changing the plants or changing their position every year. This means that it is possible to fill gaps at short notice or simply to change your mind as to the way the garden should look.

Another virtue of annuals is that they come in a wide range of colours, some of which are not so readily available in other climbers. The "hot" colours – red, orange, yellow – in partic- ular, are of great use. Annuals, on the whole, have a very long flowering season, much longer than most perennials. This also makes them very useful.

The one drawback of annuals is that they must be raised afresh each year. Many can be bought as young plants from garden centres but all can be raised from seed. This doesn't require a lot of time or space: the majority will germinate quite happily on a kitchen windowsill. With the exception of sweet peas, which are hardy and should be sown in winter, most annuals should be sown in spring, pricked out into pots, hardened off and then planted out in the open ground as soon as the threat of frosts has passed.

Annuals can be grown up any type of support, both permanent and temporary. Although they are only in place for a few months, some, such as *Cobaea scandens* (cathedral bells), can cover a very large area. Nasturtiums (*Tropaeolum*) are also annuals that can put on a lot of growth in a season.

Above: *Many climbers can be used as trailing plants as well as climbing ones. Annual nasturtiums are a good example of this. Here the nasturtium 'Jewel of Africa' is seen around a purple-leaved* Canna *'Wyoming'.*

ANNUAL CLIMBERS

Asarina	*Lagenaria* (gourds)
Caiophera	*Lathyrus odoratus* (sweet peas)
Cobaea scandens (cathedral bells)	*Lathyrus sativus*
Convolvulus tricolor	*Maurandia*
Eccremocarpus scaber	*Mikania scandens*
Ipomoea (morning glory)	*Rhodochiton atrosanguineus*
Lablab purpureus (syn. *Dolichos lablab*)	*Thunbergia alata* (black-eyed Susan)
	Tropaeolum (nasturtium)

Above: *Not all "annuals" are strictly annual.* Eccremocarpus scaber, *shown here, is really a perennial but it is often treated as an annual and planted afresh every year. It is shown with an everlasting pea,* Lathyrus latifolius.

Above: *Annuals are not restricted to just flowers. Many vegetables also make attractive climbers as well as being productive. Here, scarlet runner beans are grown up a wigwam (tepee) of canes. This is not only attractive but allows the gardener to produce quite a large crop in a small space.*

Above: *Sweet peas are amongst everyone's favourite climbers. Not only do they look good in the garden; they are also wonderful flowers for cutting for the house. Most have a delicious scent.*

Right: Cobaea scandens *is a vigorous annual climber. For success it must be planted in a warm position, preferably against a wall, and given as long a growing season as possible.*

Left: *The morning glories,* Ipomoea, *are just that, glorious. Soak seeds overnight before sowing and germinate in a warm place or propagator. Harden off thoroughly before planting or they are unlikely to do well. Plant them in a sheltered sunny position.*

Evergreen Climbers

Climbing plants are mainly valued for their flowers, but there are a few that hold their place in the garden because of their evergreen foliage. Probably the best known is ivy. Its glossy, three-pointed leaves make a permanent cover for whatever they climb up.

FOLIAGE SCREENS

One of the best uses of evergreens is as a cover for eyesores. They can be grown directly over an ugly wall or allowed to clamber over trellising judiciously positioned to hide a fuel tank or messy utility area. There are some places in the garden, moreover, where it is preferable that the appearance does not change with the seasons. A gateway, perhaps, may be surrounded by an evergreen climber over an arch, so that it presents the same familiar image to the visitor all year round.

From a design point of view, evergreen climbers provide a permanent point of reference within the garden. They form part of the structure, around which the rest of the garden changes season by season.

Plain green can be a little uninspiring; green works extremely well, however, as a backdrop against which to see other, more colourful, plants. Climbers such as ivy have glossy leaves, which reflect the light, giving a shimmering effect as they move. Evergreen leaves can vary in shape, and they can also be variegated, providing contrasting tones of green and sometimes colour variation.

Right: Laurus nobilis *provides attractive green foliage.*

EVERGREEN CLIMBERS

Clematis armandii
Clematis cirrhosa
Fremontodendron
   californicum
Hedera (ivy)
Lonicera japonica
Solanum crispum
Solanum jasminoides
Vinca major (periwinkle)

EVERGREEN WALL SHRUBS

Azara
Callistemon citrinus
Carpenteria californica
Ceanothus
Coronilla glauca
Cotoneaster
Desfontainea spinosa
Elaeagnus x ebbingei
Elaeagnus pungens
Escallonia
Euonymus fortunei
Euonymus japonicus
Garrya elliptica
Itea ilicifolia
Laurus nobilis
Magnolia grandiflora
Piptanthus laburnifolius
Pyracantha (firethorn)
Teucrium fruticans

Above: *Variegated ivies can make a big impact. Those with golden variegation are excellent for lighting up dark corners and they are especially good in helping to brighten the grey days of winter.*

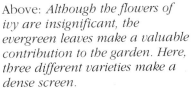

Above: *Although the flowers of ivy are insignificant, the evergreen leaves make a valuable contribution to the garden. Here, three different varieties make a dense screen.*

Right: *This* Solanum crispum *'Glasnevin' is one of the very best climbers. Unless the weather gets very cold, it retains its shiny leaves throughout the winter and then is covered with its blue flowers from late spring right through to the autumn. The leaves may drop during severe winters, but they soon recover.*

Above: Vinca major *(periwinkle) can be considered a shrub if it is kept rigorously under control by cutting back, but it is often used as a climber, scrambling through shrubs and hedges, as here. It retains its glossy green leaves throughout the winter and produces bright blue flowers from midwinter onwards.*

Below: *There is a brightly variegated periwinkle, 'Variegata', which looks good against dark hedges.*

Climbers with Spring Interest

Spring is one of the most joyous times of the year in the garden; the winter is over and ahead lie the glories of summer. Many of the plants that flower at this time of year have a freshness about them that almost defies definition.

PROTECTING FROM FROST

Spring is a time of varying weather and plants can suffer badly from late frosts. This is made worse when frosts are preceded by a warm spell, in which a lot of new growth appears. These young shoots are susceptible to sudden cold weather and can be burnt off. Buds are also likely to be harmed and it is not uncommon to see a *Clematis montana*, for example, covered in buds and full of promise one day, only to be denuded of buds the next after a night of hard frost. This, however, should never deter you from growing spring-flowering climbers; such frosts do not occur every year and, in most springs, these climbers perform at their best. If frosts are forecast, it is possible to guard against them.

Many of the more tender early-flowering shrubs need walls for protection and are usually grown as wall shrubs. Shrubs such as camellias are particularly prone to frost damage and so are grown in this way.

Once they have finished flowering, many spring-flowering climbers are a bit dreary for the rest of the year. One way to enliven them is to grow another, later-flowering, climber through their stems. This is very useful where space is limited.

SPRING-FLOWERING CLIMBERS AND WALL SHRUBS

Abeliophyllum distichum
Akebia quinata
Akebia trifoliata
Azara serrata
Ceanothus arboreus 'Trewithen Blue'
Chaenomeles (japonica or ornamental quince)
Clematis alpina
Clematis armandii
Clematis macropetala
Clematis montana
Forsythia suspensa
Garrya elliptica
Lonicera (honeysuckles)
Piptanthus laburnifolius
Ribes laurifolia
Rosa (early roses)
Schisandra
Solanum cripsum 'Glasnevin'
Wisteria

Above: *Spring is the time when all plants are beginning to burst forth. Clematis are some of the earliest climbers, one of the earliest and most impressive being* C. montana, *which frequently has so much bloom that the leaves cannot be seen.*

Right: Clematis armandii *is one of the few evergreen clematis. It is also one of the earliest to flower, doing so in late winter or early spring.*

Above: *Another early clematis, more delicate in appearance, is* C. macropetala. *It is here seen with* C. montana, *which will flower a week or so later.*

Above: *Honeysuckles* (Lonicera) *are a great feature of the spring. This one* (L. periclymenum) *is in a natural habitat – scrambling through a bush. In this case, the supporting plant is a berberis, whose purply-bronze leaves make a good contrast to the yellow flowers.*

Left: Rosa *'Maigold' is one of the many roses that although strictly a shrub, have a tendency to climb. They can be used as low climbers up pillars, as here, or on tripods, trellis or low walls. It starts flowering early in the season and often repeats later in the year.*

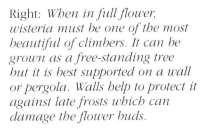

Right: *When in full flower, wisteria must be one of the most beautiful of climbers. It can be grown as a free-standing tree but it is best supported on a wall or pergola. Walls help to protect it against late frosts which can damage the flower buds.*

Climbers with Summer Interest

Summer is when many climbers are at their best. Clematis and roses, in particular, produce plenty of blooms, covering pergolas and arches as well as climbing up walls and through trees and shrubs. They make a valuable contribution to the summer scene, giving vertical emphasis to a garden that would otherwise be flat and less interesting.

SHADE AND FRAGRANCE

During hot, sunny summers, climbers are most welcome for providing dappled shade as they cover arbours and pergolas. There is nothing better than to sit on a summer's day in the shade of an arbour or relax there with a meal or a drink in the evening after work. Relaxation is further enhanced if the climbers are fragrant – and many are. Roses, honeysuckle and jasmine are three of the most popular scented climbers.

Many shrubs and trees are spring-flowering and climbers can be used to enliven them during the summer months, when they are, perhaps, at their dullest. *Clematis viticella* is probably the best to use for this purpose; because it is cut back almost to the ground during the winter, it doesn't smother the tree or shrub when it is in flower. Later in the season, when the tree or shrub has finished flowering, the clematis grows up through its branches and produces its own colour, usually over a long period.

Similarly, climbers can be used in herbaceous borders, where there are gaps left by perennials that flower early in the season and are then cut back. Clematis can be left to scramble through the border, either without any support or over a simple framework of twigs.

Above: Campsis radicans *is a beautiful climber for the second half of the summer. Its large tubular flowers, here just opening, contrast well with the green of the foliage. It is not a common climber but it is not difficult to find or to grow.*

SUMMER CLIMBERS	
Campsis	*Phaseolus coccineus* (runner beans)
Clematis	*Plumbago auriculata* (Cape leadwort)
Cobaea scandens (cathedral bells)	*Rosa* (roses)
Eccremocarpus scaber (Chilean glory flower)	*Schisandra*
Fallopia baldschuanica (Russian vine)	*Schizophragma*
Ipomoea (morning glories)	*Solanum crispum* 'Glasnevin'
Jasminum (jasmines)	*Solanum jasminoides*
Lapageria rosea	*Thunbergia alata* (black-eyed Susan)
Lathyrus (peas)	*Trachelospermum*
Lonicera (honeysuckles)	*Tropaeolum* (nasturtium)
Mutisia	*Wisteria*
Passiflora (passion-flowers)	

Above: Clematis florida *'Sieboldii' is a very distinct clematis, with creamy white outer petals and an inner button of purple ones. It is a beautiful flower even when still in bud and while opening.*

Right: Clematis *'Perle d'Azur' must be one of the best of the blue clematis. It produces flowers of a delicate lilac blue in tremendous profusion around midsummer.*

Above: *Bougainvillea is a climber from hot climates. In more temperate areas, it has to be grown under glass, such as in a conservatory, but, in warmer districts, it can be grown outside. Its brilliant colours continue for months as it is the papery bracts rather than the flowers that provide the colour.*

Right: *Scrambling plants are a neglected area. There are very many of them and they can provide a lot of vertical interest through the summer months. Here a* Euonymus fortunei *'Emerald Gaiety' scrambles up through a large bush, with* Geranium x oxonianum *pushing its way up through both.*

Left: *Unlike the sweet pea, the perennial* Lathyrus grandiflorus *does not smell, but it is a most beautiful small climber. The round pea flowers are large and full of rich colour. They are best planted under shrubs, through which they will happily scramble.*

Above: *Another scrambler is* Tropaeolum speciosum. *This, like* Lathyrus grandiflorus, *above, has a more common annual relative, the nasturtium. However,* Tropaeolum speciosum *is a perennial and has small flowers of an intense flame red. It will scramble up through any shrub.*

Right: Tropaeolum peregrinum *(canary creeper) is tender to frosts, but if protected will flower throughout the summer.*

Left: *Not-all climbers need to climb to great heights to be attractive. This herbaceous climber scrambles up through other plants with gay abandon. It is* Convolvulus althaeoides *and has delicate pink flowers, which are set off well against its silver foliage. It likes a sunny, well-drained spot.*

Above: *Passion-flowers are tender climbers, best grown against walls. Most should be grown under glass but* Passiflora caerulea *is hardy enough to be grown outside. The flowers are amongst the most extraordinary of all climbers.*

Right: *For many people, roses are the best summer climbing plants. They can be grown in a wide variety of ways, including up tripods, as seen here. This is* Rosa *'Dortmund'.*

Climbers with Autumn Interest

Most climbers have finished flowering by the time the autumn arrives but many have qualities that make them still desirable in the garden at this time of year.

FOLIAGE AND BERRIES

Perhaps the biggest attraction of autumn climbers is the change in colour of the leaves, prior to their fall. Many take on autumnal tints, some of the most fiery red. This will completely transform the appearance of the climber itself and, often, that of the surrounding area. Another benefit that some climbers have to offer is that they produce berries or fruit. Most produce seed of some kind or other but these are often visually insignificant; others produce an abundance of bright berries – honeysuckle (*Lonicera*), for example – or large luxurious fruit, such as the passion-flowers (*Passiflora*). Others carry their seeds in a different but, none the less, very attractive way. The fluffy or silky seed heads of clematis, for example, always make an interesting feature.

As well as providing an important visual element in the garden, the berries and other forms of seed are also a good source of food for birds. Birds will be attracted to the fruit for as long as they last, which may be well beyond the autumn and into the winter. Not only birds like fruit: man also likes the garden's edible bounty and many fruiting plants, ranging from currants and gooseberries to apples, plums, pears and apricots, can be grown against a wall, which provides not only support but also warmth and protection. Fruiting trees, such as apples and pears, also make good plants to train up and over arches and pergolas.

AUTUMNAL-FOLIAGED CLIMBERS

Actinidia (kiwi fruit)
Akebia quinata
Campsis
Chaenomeles (japonica or flowering quince)
Clematis alpina
Clematis flammula
Clematis tibetana vernayi
Cotoneaster
Fallopia baldschuanica (Russian vine)
Hydrangea anomala petiolaris
Hydrangea aspera
Hydrangea quercifolia
Jasminum officinale (jasmine)
Lonicera tragophylla (honeysuckle)
Parthenocissus (Boston ivy or Virginia creeper)
Passiflora (passion-flower)
Ribes speciosum
Rosa (roses)
Tropaeolum (nasturtium)
Vitis (grapevine)

BERRIED AND FRUITING CLIMBERS AND WALL SHRUBS

Actinidia (kiwi fruit)
Akebia
Clematis
Cotoneaster
Hedera (ivy)
Humulus lupulus (hop)
Ilex (holly)
Lonicera (honeysuckle)
Malus (crab apple)
Passiflora (passion-flower)
Prunus (plums, apricots, peaches)
Pyracantha (firethorn)
Pyrus (pears)
Rosa (roses)
Vitis (grapevine)

Above: Clematis cirrhosa *flowers in late autumn and carries its fluffy seed heads well into winter.*

Left: *The berries of* Cotoneaster horizontalis *are set off well against the foliage of* Helleborus foetidus.

Right: Pyracantha *offers the choice of yellow, red or orange berries, depending on the variety. This is* P. 'Orange Charmer'.

Above and right: Parthenocissus henryana *is seen here in both its summer and autumn colours.*

Left: *Clematis display a mass of silky heads as beautiful as any flowers throughout the autumn.*

Below: *Fruit trees are attractive as wall shrubs as they carry blossom in spring and fruit in the autumn. This pear, 'Doyenne du Comice', has attractive foliage, too.*

Climbers with Winter Interest

While there are not many climbers that are interesting in winter, they are still a group of plants that are worth thinking about. Valuable wall space should not be taken up with plants that do not earn their keep for the greater part of the year, but it is often possible to find space for at least one that brightens up the winter scene.

Above: Hedera colchica *'Dentata Variegata' is in perfect condition even in these frosty conditions. The gold variegation is good for lightening up dark winter days.*

Above: *The winter jasmine,* Jasminum nudiflorum, *flowers throughout winter, supplying cut flowers for indoors and decorating walls and fences outside.*

WINTER-FLOWERING CLIMBERS

Surprisingly, there is one clematis that is in full flower during the bleaker winter months. *Clematis cirrhosa* is available in several forms, some with red blotches on their bell-shaped flowers. *Clematis armandii* appears towards the end of winter and heralds the beginning of a new season. There are three honeysuckles that flower in the winter and, although they are, strictly speaking, shrubs, they can be grown against a wall. As an added bonus, these are very strongly scented and they will flower throughout the whole of the winter. Another wall shrub that flowers early is *Garrya elliptica*, with its long, silver catkins. This is the more valuable because it will grow on a north-facing wall.

One of the most commonly grown wall shrubs is the winter jasmine, *Jasminum nudiflorum*, which produces a wonderful display of bright yellow flowers. Unfortunately, unlike its summer relatives, it is not scented.

EVERGREEN CLIMBERS

While not so attractive as the flowering plants, evergreen climbers, such as ivy (*Hedera*), can be used as winter cover both for walls and for other supports. These evergreen climbers afford valuable winter protection for birds and insects, especially if grown by a warm wall. Different green tones and, especially, variegated leaves, can add a surprising amount of winter cheer, even on dark days.

Climbers and wall shrubs that still carry berries from the previous autumn can add interest in the winter. Cotoneaster and pyracantha are good examples.

WINTER CLIMBERS AND WALL SHRUBS

Chaenomeles (japonica or flowering quince)
Clematis armandii
Clematis cirrhosa
Elaeagnus x ebbingei
Elaeagnus pungens
Garrya elliptica
Hedera (ivy)
Jasminum nudiflorum (winter jasmine)
Lonicera fragrantissima (winter honeysuckle)
Lonicera x purpusii
Lonicera standishii

Right: Clematis armandii *flowers in late winter, with a wonderful display of pure-white flowers.*

Above: Garrya elliptica *is an excellent plant for winter. It has beautiful silver catkins and is one of the few plants suitable for growing on north-facing walls.*

Above: Clematis cirrhosa *is the earliest clematis to flower, starting in early winter and continuing until spring. The many varieties include this one, 'Balearica'.*

Right: Chaenomeles, *known as* japonica, *or Japanese or ornamental quince, flowers from midwinter to spring, then has hard fruit that often lasts through until the next spring.*

Fragrant Climbers

When choosing plants, the main consideration is, often, what the flowers are like, followed by the foliage. Something that is often forgotten, or just considered as a bonus, is fragrance; and yet it is something that most people enjoy and it enhances the pleasure of all uses of the garden.

USING FRAGRANCE

Climbers include some of the loveliest and most scented plants in the garden. Some of them, such as honeysuckle or jasmine, will perfume the air over a long distance. They are always worth growing on house walls near windows that are often open, so that the beautiful smells waft in and fill the rooms. Another good place to locate fragrant climbers is over an arbour or where there is a seat. Fragrance can be a tremendous aid to relaxation: just think about the idea of sitting in the evening, after a hard day, with the air filled with the smell of honeysuckle, for example.

Most scented climbers are at their best in the evening. This is a bonus if you are at work all day and, again, makes them very suitable for planting where you relax or have your evening meal. Some scented climbers, such as sweet peas, make ideal flowers for cutting to bring indoors.

Check carefully that a climber is fragrant. Honeysuckles (*Lonicera*) are amongst the most fragrant of climbers, but not all of them are scented, by any means. *Lonicera tragophylla* and *L. × tellmanniana* are both very attractive honeysuckles, but neither has any smell at all. Roses, too, vary in the intensity of their scent, and it is worth finding out which ones you like

best. Another thing to be beware of is that not all smells are nice. The privets (*Ligustrum*), which are sometimes used as wall shrubs, have a smell that many people find revolting.

FRAGRANT CLIMBERS AND WALL SHRUBS

Azara
Clematis montana
Itea ilicifolia
Jasminum (jasmine)
Lathyrus odoratus (sweet peas)
Lonicera (honeysuckle)
Magnolia grandiflora
Osmanthus
Passiflora (passion-flower)
Rosa (roses)

Above: *The fragrance of this* Rosa *'Wedding Day' climbing through a tree will be carried far in the warm summer evenings.*

Above: *Honeysuckle has a very heady perfume, from flowers that first appear in spring and then continue through the summer; odd flowers are still being produced in autumn.*

Left: *Not all honeysuckles are fragrant but* Lonicera periclymenum *and its varieties are amongst the best. They can be vigorous growers and need strong supports.*

Above: *Growing Rosa 'Zéphirine Drouhin' around a summer house is ideal. This rose has a delightful perfume and flowers on and off throughout the summer and well into the autumn. It has the advantage that it is thornless and so is safe to use near places where people are sitting or walking.*

Above: *Jasmine has a very distinctive fragrance and is most appreciated on a warm summer evening. This variety, Jasminum officinale 'Aureum', has gold-splashed leaves. This gives the climber an attraction even when it is out of flower.*

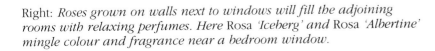

Right: *Roses grown on walls next to windows will fill the adjoining rooms with relaxing perfumes. Here Rosa 'Iceberg' and Rosa 'Albertine' mingle colour and fragrance near a bedroom window.*

Wall Shrubs

Not all plants that one sees climbing up walls or supported on trellis are true climbers. Many are just ordinary shrubs that are growing against a wall for a variety of reasons. In the wild, some of these might scramble through others if they are next to them, but, generally, they are free-standing shrubs. These shrubs are used as surrogate climbers in the garden, partly because they look good in positions where climbers are grown and partly because some need the protection that walls and fences provide.

ADVANTAGES OF WALL SHRUBS

From the design point of view, wall shrubs are often more compact and controllable than climbers. They can be used in smaller spaces, which climbers would soon outgrow. If so desired, they can be clipped into topiary shapes and they will retain their shape for some time, unlike climbers, which have a constant tendency to throw out new shoots. Wall shrubs increase the range of flowering colours and periods available to the gardener, as well as offering a greater range of foliage effects.

Walls offer winter protection to many shrubs that could otherwise not be grown. The warmth that comes from a house wall might horrify the conservationally minded but, to the gardener, it offers the opportunity to grow plants, such as *Ceanothus*, which might otherwise succumb to the cold weather and die.

It is sometimes difficult to tell what is a climber and what is a wall shrub. *Pyracantha* cut tight against a wall, for example, has every appearance of being a climber, as has a large *Magnolia grandiflora*. *Euonymus fortunei*, which grows like any other shrub in the open ground, will, given the chance, shin up a wall as if that were its normal habitat. But, in fact, the difference between climbers and wall shrubs does not matter. Most gardeners are concerned about the appearance of the garden and are not worried about categories. Sad would be the case if a plant were banished from a wall or some other support simply because it was not, strictly speaking, a climber.

Above: Piptanthus nepalensis *blooms in the spring, producing bright yellow, pea-like flowers. As summer moves on, so these attractive pods are formed, adding yet another dimension to the plant. Both the flowers and pods show up well against a brick wall.*

Left: Fremontodendron californicum *is usually grown against a wall. Wear a mask when pruning or handling as the stems are covered with fine hairs that can get into the lungs.*

Right: *Although most frequently used as a free-standing shrub,* Euonymus fortunei *'Emerald 'n' Gold' will happily climb up a wall or fence.*

Above: Carpenteria californica *is one of the glories of the summer, with its large white flowers, surmounted by a boss of yellow stamens. These are set off well by the dark green foliage. This plant is usually grown as a wall shrub, because it is slightly tender and appreciates the protection of the wall.*

Left: Calistemon citrinus, *with its curious, bottle-brush-like flowers, is a tender shrub that needs the warm protection of a wall if it is to survive. It flowers during the summer months.*

Above: Ceanothus *produces some of the best blue flowers of any wall shrubs. Many can be grown free-standing, but most do best if grown against a wall or a fence as here.*

TRAINING CLIMBERS

Training Methods 1

Training is an important aspect of growing climbers. The general shape and well-being of the plant is taken care of by pruning, but how it is trained and where it is positioned are the most important things to consider when thinking about how your climber will look.

POSITIONING THE PLANT

The overall shape of the plant depends on its position. Those against a wall, for example, need to be tied in so that they do not protrude too far. Similarly, climbers over arches must be constrained on at least the inner side, so that they do not catch people walking through the arch. In some places, the plants can be left to show off the way they froth out over their supports. Vigorous climbers covering large trees, for example, are best left natural and untrained. Plants on trellis can be allowed a certain amount of ebullient freedom but they may also need some restraint.

SPREADING OUT THE STEMS

The climber's natural tendency is to go straight up through its support or host until it reaches the light. This frequently means that the climber forms a tight column without much deviation on either side. To make a good display the gardener should spread out the stems at as early a stage as possible so that the main stems fan out, covering the wall, fence or trellis. This not only means that the climber covers a wider area but also that its stems all receive a good amount of light, and thus flowering is encouraged at a lower level.

EARLY DAYS

At the time of planting it can be a good policy to train individual stems along canes until they reach the wires, trellis or whatever the support may be. This will prevent them from all clustering together, making it difficult to train them at a later stage. Once the plant starts to put on growth, tie this in rather than tucking it behind the trellis or wires. This will enable you to release it at a later stage to re-organize it.

Above: *Tying in climbers under overhanging tiles can be a problem, because it may be difficult to find anchor points. A criss-cross arrangement of vertical wires can normally be fixed between the end of the eaves and the wall below the tiles; it makes an attractive feature in its own right. Here, Rosa 'Zéphirine Drouhin' is supported on wires.*

Right: *Horizontal training produces some of the best flowering. Here, Rosa 'Seagull' has been trained along swags of rope suspended between wooden pillars. Do not pull the ropes too tight: a graceful curve gives a much better effect. If it is not self-clinging, tie the climber in well to the rope or it will become loose and thrash about.*

Above: *A similar effect to climbing on ropes can be had by training the climber along poles attached to pillars. These form a rustic trellis and can look very effective, even during the winter when the climber is not in leaf Here,* Rosa *'Felicia' clambers over the structure.*

Right: *Vigorous climbers, such as rambling roses, some clematis and Russian vines, can be grown through trees. This is an easy way of training because, once the plant has been pointed in the right direction (by tying it to a cane angled into the tree), it can be left to its own devices. Make certain that the tree can support the weight of the climber, especially in high winds. Here* Rosa *'Paul's Himalayan Musk' begins its ascent.*

Training Methods 2

ENCOURAGING FLOWERS

Once the climber has thrown up some nice long shoots, bend these over in a curving arc and attach them to the wires or trellis. From these will come new shoots which should be treated in the same manner so that the wall, fence or trellis is covered in a increasing series of arching stems. This method has the advantage, besides creating a good coverage of the wall, of making the plant produce plenty of flowers. The chemistry of the stems is such that flower buds are laid down on the top edge of the curving branches. Roses, in particular, benefit greatly from this method of training.

Curving branches over to encourage growth can also be used for climbers growing around tripods or round a series of hooped sticks, where the stems are tied around the structure rather than in a vertical position. This will encourage a much thicker coverage and many more blooms as well as allowing you to use vigorous plants in a limited amount of space.

CHOOSING YOUR METHOD OF TRAINING

There are endless possibilities for training your climber, and really the choice will affected by the constraints of the garden and personal choice. You may have something particular in mind – for example, you may want to construct a shady arbour or romantic walkway – or you may have simply bought a climber you took a fancy to and now want to find a good place for it where it will flourish and add to the beauty of the garden.

TRAINING CLIMBERS OVER EYESORES

Climbers that grow quickly and produce lots of flowers are well-suited to covering unsightly features in the garden such as refuse areas, grey concrete walls belonging to a neighbouring property or ugly fences you are not allowed to pull down.

CLIMBERS TO TRAIN OVER EYESORES

Clematis montana
Clematis rehderiana
Fallopia baldschuanica (Russian vine)
Hedera (ivy)
Humulus (hops)
Hydrangea anomala petiolaris
Lonicera (honeysuckles)
Rosa (roses)

CLIMBERS AND WALL SHRUBS FOR NORTH- AND EAST-FACING WALLS

Akebia quinata
Camellia
Chaenomeles (Japonica or ornamental quince)
Clematis 'Marie Boisselot'
Clematis 'Nelly Moser'
Euonymous fortunei
Jasminum nudiflorum
Hedera (Ivy)
Hydrangea anomala petiolaris
Lonicera x tellemanniana
Parthenocissus (Boston ivy or virginia creeper)
Pyracantha (Firethorn)
Rosa 'New Dawn'
Schizophragma

Above: Rosa *'New Dawn' has a very long flowering period and has the added benefit that it can be grown on a north-facing wall. Here it has been tied into trellising on a wall.*

Left: *Climbers planted near doorways should be kept under control to avoid injury. Clematis, such as this C. 'Rouge Cardinal', are safer than roses as they have no thorns to catch the unwary.*

Above: *When roses are well-trained they can produce an abundance of flowers. The curiously coloured R. 'Veilchenblau', shown here growing up a wooden trellis, puts on a fine show during midsummer.*

Above: *If possible, train climbers that have scented flowers near open windows, so that their fragrance can be appreciated indoors. Here Rosa 'Albertine' is in full flower, while beyond is a wisteria that has finished flowering.*

Right: *To obtain extra height for the more vigorous roses a trellis can be erected on top of a wall. When well-trained they present a backdrop of colour against which to view the border in front and below.*

Growing Climbers on Wires

If a large area of wall is to be covered with non-clinging climbers, wires are the only realistic way of supporting them. Alternative methods, such as covering the whole wall with wooden trellis, are expensive and, if the wall is at all attractive, may detract from its appearance.

HOW TO USE WIRES

Wires can be used for most types of climbers, except for clinging ones, which should be able to cling directly to the surface of the wall. If the wires are too far apart, however, plants with tendrils may have difficulty finding the next wire up and may need to be tied in. Wires are also suitable for wall shrubs, which while not needing support, benefit from being tied in to prevent them from being blown forward by wind rebounding from the wall. Wires are unobtrusive and can be painted the same colour as the wall, to make them even less visible. Galvanized wire is best, as it will not rust. Rusty wires are not only liable to break but may also cause unsightly rust marks that may show up on the wall. Plastic-covered wire can be used but the coating is not as permanent as a galvanized one.

Do not use too thin a wire or it will stretch under the weight of the plants. If there is a chance that the wires will stretch, use bottle screws or tension bolts at one end. These can be tightened as the wire slackens.

1 Before it is fixed to wires, the young plant is loose and growing in all directions.

2 The wires are supported by vine eyes, which are fastened into the wall. Although you might be able to hammer them directly into soft brickwork, it is usually easier to drill a pilot hole.

3 If you are using vine eyes with a screw fixing, you need to insert a plastic or wooden plug in the wall first. The eye is then screwed into the plug. This type of vine eye varies in length, the long ones being necessary for those climbers, such as wisteria, that grow large and need wires further from the wall.

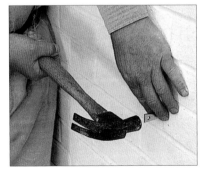

4 The simplest vine eyes are wedge shaped. Hammer them directly into the masonry and then feed the wire through a hole. While wedge-shaped eyes are suitable for brick and stone walls, the screw type are better for wooden fences and posts.

5 Thread the galvanized wire through the hole in the vine eye and wrap it round itself, forming a firm fixing. Thread the other end through the intermediate eyes (set at no more than 180 cm/6 ft intervals and preferably closer) and then fasten the wire round the end eye, keeping it as taut as possible.

6 Curve over the long stems and attach them to the wires, using either plastic ties or string. Tie at several points, if necessary, so that the stems lie flat against the wall and do not flap about.

7 When all the stems are tied in, you should have a series of arches. Tying them in like this, rather than straight up the wall, covers the wall better and encourages the plant to produce flowering buds all along the top edge of the stems.

Above: *Climbers such as roses and clematis can be trained up the whole side of a house with wires. Here* Rosa *'Madame Isaac Pereire' completely covers its wires.*

Fixing Trellis to Walls

Permanent wooden trellis, fixed to a wall, is not only a strong method of supporting climbers but also an attractive one. However, large areas of trellis can look overpowering, especially on house walls; wires are a better choice for these situations. Apart from self-clinging plants, which support themselves, any type of climber can be held up by such trellis.

HOW TO USE TRELLIS

The trellis should be well fixed to the wall, preferably with screws. It should be held a short distance from the brickwork or masonry, so that the stems of the climber can easily pass up behind it. This can be simply achieved by using spacers – wooden blocks will do – between the trellis and the wall.

If the wall is a painted one, or might need future attention for other reasons, it is possible to make the trellis detachable. The best method is to fix hinges along the bottom edge of the trellis. This allows the framework to be gently eased away from the wall, bringing the climber with it, so that maintenance can take place. The top is held by a catch. Alternatively, the trellis can be held in position by a series of clips or catches. This is not so easy to manoeuvre as one held on hinges, however.

Any shape of trellis can be used, such as square, rectangular or fan shaped, depending on the climber and the effect of the shape on the building or wall. It is possible to be more imaginative and devise other shapes, perhaps creating a two-dimensional topiary. The mesh can be either square or diagonal, the former being better with brickwork, because the lines of the trellis then follow those of the brick courses rather than contradicting them.

CLIMBERS FOR TRELLIS

Akebia
Clematis
Cobaea scandens (cathedral bells)
Humulus (hop)
Ipomoea (morning glory)
Lathyrus odoratus (sweet peas)
Lonicera (honeysuckle)
Rosa (roses)
Solanum crispum
Solanum jasminoides
Thunbergia alata (black-eyed Susan)

1 Take the trellis to the wall and mark its position. Drill holes for fixing the spacers and insert plastic or wooden plugs.

2 Drill the equivalent holes in the wooden batten and secure it to the wall, checking with a spirit level that it is horizontal. Use a piece of wood that holds the trellis at least 2.5 cm (1 in) from the wall. Fix a similar batten at the base and one half-way up for trellis above 1.2 m (4 ft) high.

3 Drill and screw the trellis to the battens, first fixing the top and then working downwards. Check that the trellis is not crooked.

4 The finished trellis should be tightly fixed to the wall, so that the weight of the climber, and any wind that blows on it, will not pull it away from its fixings.

Above: *The rose 'Dublin Bay' here climbs up a wooden trellis secured to the wall. This rose is fragrant and flowers over a very long period.*

Growing Climbers on Netting

A cheap but effective method of providing support for climbers on a wall is to use a rigid plastic netting. This can be used for large areas but it is more effective for smaller climbers, where a limited area is covered.

HOW TO USE NETTING

Rigid plastic netting is suitable for covering brick or stone walls as well as wooden walls and panel fences. It can also be wrapped around poles or pillars, to give plants something to grip. You can string netting between upright posts, as a temporary support for annual climbing plants such as sweet peas, but it is not really suitable for a permanent structure of this sort.

Netting is readily available from garden centres and nurseries. It can generally be bought in green, brown or white, which allows you to choose a colour that matches the wall, so that the netting does not show up too obviously. It is also possible to buy special clips, which make fixing the netting to a surface very simple.

The clips are designed to be used either with masonry nails or with screws. They have the advantage that they hold the netting away from the wall, so that there is room for the plant to climb through it or wrap its tendrils round the mesh, whereas if the netting is nailed directly to the wall there is no space between them.

A further advantage of this method of fixing is that the net can be unclipped and eased away from the wall, allowing the latter to be painted or treated with preservative before the net is clipped back into position.

Plastic netting can be used either with plants that support themselves with tendrils or by twining, or with plants that need to be tied in. It does not look as attractive as the more expensive wooden trellising but, once it has been covered with the climber, it is not noticeable, especially if the right colour has been chosen. After a few years you will not be able to see the netting at all; it will be covered in a mass of foliage and flowers.

1 Position the first clip just below the top of where the net will be and drive in a masonry nail. Alternatively, drill a hole, plug it and screw the clip into it.

2 With a spirit level, mark the position of the other upper clip, so that it is level with the first. Fix the second clip.

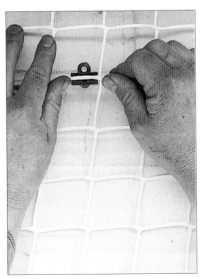

3 Place the top of the net in position, with one horizontal strand in the jaw of the clip. Press it home so it is securely fastened. Repeat with the other clip.

4 Smooth the net down against the wall and mark where the next set of clips will come. They should be at about 60 cm (2 ft) intervals down the wall. Move the net out of the way, fix the clips and press the net into the clips. Follow the same procedure with the bottom clips.

5 When the netting is securely in place, train the climber up into it. Even those that are self-supporting may need tying in to get them going. If the plant is a little way out from the wall, train it towards the netting along canes.

Above: *Netting is rather ugly and it is best used with vigorous climbers that will soon cover it. Here, the netting has only been used well above the ground, where the main support is needed. Unsightly supports won't show around the base of the climbers, where the main stems make an attractive feature in their own right.*

Trellis and Fences

One of the simplest and yet most decorative ways of displaying climbers is to grow them over free-standing trellises or fences. Used in the garden, to define its major routes, this is an impressive way of bringing planting right in to the garden's fundamental structure.

BOUNDARIES AND SCREENS

Fences tend to be functional, in that they create a boundary; this is usually between the garden and the outside world but a fence is sometimes used as an internal divider. Many existing fences are ugly and covering them with climbers is a good way of hiding this fact. Those erected by the gardener need not be ugly but they still provide an opportunity for climbers.

Trellises are usually much more decorative than fences. They are not so solid and allow glimpses of what lies on the other side. They are either used as internal dividers within the garden, as screens, or simply as a means of supporting climbers. Used in this way, trellis can make a tremendous contribution to a garden design, as they can provide horizontal as well as vertical emphasis. As screens, they are useful for disguising eyesores such as fuel tanks, garages or utility areas.

ERECTING TRELLIS

The key to erecting a good trellis is to make certain that it is firmly planted in the ground. Once covered with climbers, it will come under enormous pressure from the wind and will work loose unless firmly embedded in concrete. Do not try to take a short cut by simply back-filling the post-hole with earth; unless the trellis is in a very protected position, it will eventually fall over. Panel fences are erected in a similar way.

Virtually any climber can be grown over trellis. But unless it is in a sheltered position, trellis will not offer the same protection as a wall to tender climbers.

1 Dig a hole at least 60 cm (2 ft) deep, deeper in light soils.

2 Put the post in the prepared hole and partly fill the hole with a dry-mix concrete. Check that the post is upright and not sloping, using a spirit level. Adjust the position of the post, if necessary, and then continue filling the hole, tamping down firmly as you go to hold the pole still.

3 Continue filling the hole with concrete, ramming it down firmly; frequently check that the post is still upright. The post should now be firm enough in the ground to work on and, once the concrete has "cured", it will be permanently secure.

4 Lay the panel on the ground, to work out where the next hole should be. Dig the hole, again to at least 60 cm (2 ft) deep.

5 Nail the panel on to the first post, while a helper supports the free end.

6 Place the second post in its hole and nail it to the panel, checking that the tops of the posts are level and the panel is horizontal. Fill the second hole with dry-mix concrete, tamping it down as you proceed. Check that the post is upright and adjust, if necessary.

7 Repeat the steps by digging the third post hole, nailing on the second panel, positioning and nailing the third post and so on, until the length of trellising is complete. This is more accurate than putting in all the posts and then fixing the panels, when, inevitably, some gaps will be too large and some too small.

Above: *Honeysuckles will quickly cover trellis.*

Hoops

Training over hoops allows you to direct the growth of the plant, so that it covers all the available space. If the plant is allowed to shoot heavenwards, the result can be disappointing, whereas, if you spread out the initial stems at the base when you first plant, you can encourage the plant to make a much better display.

THE AIMS OF TRAINING

Bending the new young growth into curving arches encourages flowering buds to be formed along the whole length of the stem, rather than just at the tip, as happens if the branch is tied in a vertical position. Frequently, new shoots will also develop from the curving stems and these should, in turn, also be tied into an arch, gradually encouraging the climber to cover the whole

hoop. This will encourage a much thicker coverage and many more blooms.

Training plants over hoops helps keep their final height in proportion to the border in which they are growing. It is a very useful method for growing reasonably vigorous plants in a limited space. Very vigorous plants are best avoided; they will soon outgrow their space, however much training you do!

1 In early spring, make a series of hoops around the rose, pushing each end of the pole into the ground. The wood used should be pliable, hazel (Corylus avellana) being one of the best to use. Bend each stem carefully, so that it does not crack.

2 Allow each hoop to overlap the previous one.

3 Sort out the long shoots of the rose, carefully bend them over and then tie them to a convenient point on the hoop. In some cases, it may be easier to tie the shoot to a stem that has already been tied down.

4 To start with, the "bush" will look rather untidy but, gradually, the leaves will turn to face the light and it will produce new buds all along the upper edges of the curved stems.

5 Gradually the plant will fill out, and by midsummer it should be a mass of blooms. Every year, remove a few of the older stems and tie in all new ones. After a few years, remove the old hoops and replace them with new ones.

Above: *Roses grown over hoops form a dense bush that is covered with flowers. Here R. 'Isphahan' puts on a good display of flowers as well as putting on plenty of new growth for the following year.*

Growing Climbers up Tripods

Tripods provide a useful opportunity for growing climbers in borders and other areas of limited space. A tripod helps to create vertical emphasis in gardens and may become a striking focal point if eye-catching climbers are allowed to cover it with foliage and flowers.

USING TRIPODS

Tripods can be formal, made to a classic design, or they can be made from rustic poles. The former are better where they are still partly on show after the climber is in full growth. The latter, on the other hand, in spite of their rustic and informal charm, are more suitable for carrying heavy, rampant climbers that will cover them completely. Tripods provide a more substantial support than a single pole.

More formal designs can be bought complete, ready to be installed in the garden. Tripods can, of course, also be made by the competent woodworker. A rustic-pole tripod is much more basic and can easily be constructed by most gardeners. They can be made to any height, to suit the eventual height of the plants and the visual aspects of the site.

Although any type of climber can be grown up a tripod, self-clingers would not be so good because there isn't enough flat surface for them to attach their modified roots. Tripods are ideal for carrying two or more climbers at once. If possible, choose climbers that flower at different times. Alternatively, choose two that flower at the same time but look particularly well together.

An ideal combination is a rose and a *Clematis viticella*. The latter is pruned almost to the ground each winter and so is still growing while the rose is in flower and, therefore, does not smother it. Later in the summer, the clematis comes into its own when the rose is past its best.

1 Position three posts in the ground. The distance apart will depend on the height; balance the two to get a good shape. The posts can be driven into the ground but a better job is done if you dig holes at least 60 cm (2 ft) deep. For a really solid job, backfill the holes with dry-mix concrete, but it will normally be sufficient just to ram the earth back around the poles.

2 Nail cross-pieces between the posts. These will not only help support the plants but also give the structure rigidity. Rails at 40–45 cm (15–18 in) apart should be sufficient for tying in stems. If you want more support for self-clingers, wrap a layer of wire netting around the structure. The plants will soon hide it.

3 When you nail the cross-pieces to the poles, the ends may well split if they have already been cut to the exact length. Nail the pieces on first and then cut them to the right length. Alternatively, cut to length and then drill holes in the appropriate places before nailing to the poles.

4 Plant the climbers in and around the tripod. Avoid planting them too close to the upright poles as the earth here will either be rammed down hard or have been replaced with concrete. Before planting, dig in some well-rotted organic material.

5 Water all the plants in well. If the weather continues dry, keep watering until the plants have become established. Always soak the ground well: a dribble on the surface will not help the plants send roots out into the surrounding soil.

6 The finished tripod will look a bit raw at first but it will soon weather and become covered in plants.

CLIMBERS SUITABLE FOR TRIPODS
Clematis
Humulus (hop)
Lonicera (honeysuckle)
Rosa (roses)
Solanum jasminoides
Tropaeolum (nasturtiums)
Vitis (vines)

Right: *As an alternative, a tripod can be constructed so that the tops meet, forming a three-sided pyramid. Here, Clematis 'Jackmanii' is seen clambering up such a design; once fully grown, the clematis will cover the support completely, so that the tripod cannot be seen.*

Simple Pillars for Climbers

A very effective way of displaying climbers is to grow them up a single pole, which is usually called a pillar. This can look very elegant and also means it is possible to grow a large number of climbers in a relatively small space. Pillars create vertical emphasis in borders or small gardens, without creating a barrier.

CLIMBERS FOR PILLARS

Clematis
Humulus (hop)
Lonicera (honeysuckle)
Rosa (roses)
Solanum jasminoides
Tropaeolum (nasturtiums)
Vitis (vines)

USING PILLARS

A surprising number of climbers are suited to growing up pillars. Most climbing roses, for example, look particularly good growing up them, although it is probably best to avoid vigorous climbers or rambling roses.

An advantage of using pillars for your climbers is that they are inexpensive and simple to erect and take down.

The pillar shown here is permanently positioned in a border but is possible to place the posts in a collar of concrete or a metal tube, so that they can be taken down during the winter when they are bare.

Movable columns are best suited to annuals or *Clematis viticella*, which can be cut down almost to the ground before the posts are removed. Permanent climbers, such as roses, will need a permanent structure.

If space is available, a very attractive walkway can be created by using a series of pillars along a path. This can be further improved by connecting the tops with rope, along which swags of climbers can grow. This is a very good way of growing roses and creates a very romantic, fragrant route through the garden. The effect is suited to formal designs, but is so soft and flowing that it gives a very relaxing feel.

1 Dig a hole at least 60 cm (2 ft) deep. Put in the post and check that it is upright. Backfill with earth, ramming it firmly down as it is filled. In exposed gardens, a more solid pillar can be created by filling the hole with concrete.

2 Plants can be tied directly to the post but a more natural support is created if wire netting is secured to the post. Plants such as clematis will then be able to climb by themselves with little attention from you other than tying in wayward stems.

3 Plant the climber a little way out from the pole, to avoid the compacted area. Lead the stems to the wire netting and tie them in, to get them started. Self-clingers will now take over but plants such as roses will need to be tied in as they climb. Twining plants, such as hops, can be grown up the pole without the wire.

Left: Clematis 'W.E. Gladstone' climbing up a pillar. If the pole was covered with wire netting the plant would have more to grip on, which would prevent it suddenly collapsing down the pole under its own weight as it may do later here.

Right: Although single-post pillars are rather slim, they can accommodate more than one climber. Here there are two roses, 'American Pillar' and 'Kew Rambler'. Another option is to choose one rose and a later-flowering clematis.

Above: Single-post pillars help to break up what would, otherwise, be a dull, rather two-dimensional border. Although it is only a thin structure, when clothed with a climber it becomes a well-filled-out, irregular shape, as this 'American Pillar' rose shows.

Growing Climbers Through Trees and Shrubs

In the wild, many climbing plants that are also used in the garden find support by scrambling up through trees and shrubs. In thick woodland or forests, they may grow to 50 m (150 ft) plus, in search of light. In the garden, supports of this height are rarely available, and, if they were, the flowers of the climbers using them would be out of sight.

CHOOSING GOOD PARTNERS

A smaller support is required for cultivated climbers in the garden, with a large apple tree, therefore, usually being the highest used. Clematis and roses will scramble through the branches, creating huge fountains of flowers. On a more modest scale, even dwarf shrubs can be used to support some low-growing climbers.

One of the advantages of growing climbers through shrubs is that it is possible to obtain two focuses of interest in one area. This is particularly true of early-flowering shrubs, which are relatively boring for the rest of the year. Through these, it is possible to train a later-flowering climber to enliven the area further on in the season. Clematis are particularly good for this, especially the later-flowering forms, such as the viticellas. These can be cut nearly to the ground during the winter, so that the shrub is relatively uncluttered with the climber when it is in flower itself earlier on in the next season.

Fruit trees that have finished their fruiting life can be given new appeal if you grow a rose through them. However, it is important to remember that old trees may be weak and that the extra burden of a large rose, especially in a high wind, may be too much for it to carry.

CLIMBERS SUITABLE FOR GROWING THROUGH TREES
Akebia
Clematis
Fallopia baldschuanica
  (Russian vine)
Humulus (hop)
Lonicera (honeysuckle)
Rosa (roses – vigorous varieties)
Solanum crispum
Solanum jasminoides

CLIMBERS SUITABLE FOR GROWING THROUGH SHRUBS
Clematis
Cobaea scandens (cathedral
  bells)
Eccremocarpus scaber (Chilean
  glory flower)
Ipomoea (morning glory)
Lathyrus odoratus
  (sweet peas)
Thunbergia alata (black-eyed
  Susan)
Tropaeolum (nasturtiums)
Vinca major

1 Any healthy shrub or tree can be chosen. It should preferably be one that flowers at a different time to the climber. Choose companions that will not swamp each other. Here, a relatively low *Salix helvetica* is to be planted with a small form of *Clematis alpina*. The two will make a delicate mix, especially the blue clematis flowers against the silver foliage of the *Salix helvetica*.

2 Dig the planting area at a point on the perimeter of the shrub and prepare the soil by adding well-rotted organic material. For clematis, choose a position on the shady side of the plant, so that its roots are in shade but the flowers will be up in the sun. Dig a hole bigger than the climber's rootball and plant it. Most climbers should be planted at the same depth as they were in their pots but clematis should be 5 cm (2 in) or so deeper.

3 Using a cane, train the clematis into the bush. Once the clematis has become established, you can remove the cane. Spread the shoots of the climber out so that it spreads evenly through the shrub, not just in one area.

4 If possible, put the climber outside the canopy of the shrub or tree, so that it receives rain. However, it is still important to water in the new plant and, should the weather be dry, to continue watering until the plant is established.

Above: *The beautiful white clematis 'Marie Boisselot' grows up through a small apple tree.*

Archways

Arches are very versatile features in a garden and are well suited for growing a variety of climbers. Archways can be incorporated into a dividing feature, such as a wall, hedge or fence, or can be free-standing along a path as nothing more than a means of supporting climbers.

USING ARCHES

Archways exert a magnetic effect on visitors to your garden. No matter how interesting the area you are in, an archway draws the eye to what lies beyond. It creates mystery with tantalizing glimpses of other things.

Those forming entrances are important features. They are often the first thing that a visitor is aware of on entering a garden. Arches frame the scene beyond and create atmosphere. A cottage garden, for example, looks particularly fine when seen through a rose arch, while a formal town garden may be better suited to a simple arch of foliage, such as ivy.

The possibilities of creating an arch are almost endless. They can be purchased in kit form, made to order or made by the gardener. They can be made from metal, wood, brick or stone work. Plastic ones are also available, but are neither very attractive nor long lasting. Wooden ones present the biggest range. They can be formal ones created from panels of trellis, or informal ones made from rustic poles. The choice is normally limited by cost and the appearance that is required – climbers themselves will generally climb over anything.

Always choose or make one that is big enough for people to walk through when it is fully clad with climbers – which may stick out as far as 60 cm (2 ft) or more from the supports. Make certain that the supports are well sunk into the ground, preferably concreted in. When covered with a voluminous climber, an arch may be under great pressure from the wind and a storm may push over a badly constructed one, destroying your display.

Virtually any climbers can be used with archways, although over-vigorous ones can become a nuisance – they seem to be constantly growing across the entrance itself. Other types of climbers to avoid, unless there is plenty of room, are thorned roses which may cause injury, or coarse-stemmed plants such as hops. These can be dangerous to the unwary. If you want a rose, use something like 'Zéphirine Drouhin', which is thornless.

CLIMBERS FOR ARCHWAYS

Akebia
Campsis radicans
Clematis
Phaseolus (climbing beans)
Humulus (hop)
Lonicera (honeysuckle)
Rosa (roses)
Vitis (vines)

Above: *A simple arch, constructed from rustic poles and covered with a variegated ivy. The simplicity of the foliage allows the eye to pass through to the garden beyond, without distraction.*

Above: *Wisteria makes a good covering for an arch because, once it has finished flowering, its foliage still retains a great deal of interest. It is accompanied here by* Vitis coignetiae, *whose foliage turns a magnificent purple colour in autumn. Together, these climbers provide interest from spring to autumn.*

Above: *A golden hop,* Humulus lupulus aureus, *and a honeysuckle,* Lonicera periclymenum, *combine to decorate this archway. Again, interest should be provided from spring to autumn.*

Above left: *This wonderfully romantic arch seems to come from the middle of nowhere. The roses and long grass create a soft image that provides nothing but delight.*

Left: *Roses make excellent subjects for archways. Repeat-flowering ones provide the longest interest; once-flowering roses can be combined with late-flowering clematis, to extend the season.*

Arbours

An arbour is a framework over which climbers are trained to create a shady outdoor room. It can be just big enough to take a chair or bench, but best of all is an arbour large enough to accommodate a table and several chairs, where you can sit and linger over alfresco meals.

CLIMBERS FOR ARBOURS

Clematis (some fragrant)
Fallopia baldschuanica (Russian vine – very vigorous)
Hedera (ivy – evergreen)
Humulus (hop – dies back in winter)
Lonicera (honeysuckle – many fragrant)
Rosa (roses – many fragrant)
Vitis (vines – some fruiting)

DESIGNING AN ARBOUR

The structure can be of metal or wood or the arbour can have brick or stone piers with a wooden roof. The design can be any shape that takes the fancy or fits the site. It may be triangular, semi-circular, rectangular or octagonal, to suggest but a few. The climbers can be any that you like. If you do not like bees, stick to climbers grown for their foliage. In areas designed for relaxation, fragrant climbers are most welcome. Honeysuckle provides a delicious scent, particularly in the evening. Jasmine is another good evening plant. For daytime enjoyment, fragrant roses are ideal.

An arbour may have to remain in place for many years, so make sure you build it well. Take trouble to use timbers treated with preservative (not creosote, which may kill many climbers) and make certain that it is a strong design, well supported in the ground. As with similar structures covered in heavy climbers, the wind can wreak havoc on weak construction.

Right: *Here, the overhanging fig,* Ficus carica, *and the surrounding rose, clematis and other climbers create an intimate area for sitting and relaxing, which fulfils all the functions of an arbour, even though there is no supporting structure.*

Above: *This arbour is dappled with shade from a number of roses. It is big enough for small supper parties as well as simply sitting in the evening with a drink.*

Above: *A large arbour, built for entertaining, this example is covered in a variety of climbers, including a purple grapevine. This provides a wonderfully dappled shade, as well as colourful foliage and grapes at the end of the autumn. Clematis montana supplies the colour in the spring and early summer.*

Above: *A dual-purpose arbour: the newly planted beans will provide shade during the hotter part of the year, as well as a constant supply of runner beans for the kitchen. As a bonus, the flowers provide an added attraction.*

Walkways and Pergolas

Extending the use of arches and trellis brings the possibility of pergolas and walkways. This is an ideal way of providing a shady path. On the whole, these are not suitable for the smaller garden, although it is surprising what can be achieved with a bit of imagination.

USING WALKWAYS AND PERGOLAS

Walkways are open pergolas, with no roof. They can be double-sided, that is, down both sides of a path, or you can use a single piece of trellis down one side. The simplest way is to build them out of either trellis or rustic poles. For a romantic version, use a series of pillars linked with swags of ropes.

Both can become massive structures that have to support a great deal of weight, especially when there is a strong wind blowing, so it is important to make certain that, whatever the material, the walkway or pergola is well constructed.

A wide range of climbing plants can be used to clothe the pergola or walkway; fragrant plants are especially pleasing. Roses are ideal, as long as they are either thornless or well tied in so that they do not catch passers-by with their thorns. Evergreen climbers, such as ivy, make a dark and intriguing tunnel and will keep passers-by dry in wet weather throughout the year.

Right: *An arch leads through into another part of the garden. The poles are covered with* Rosa 'American Pillar' *and* R. 'Albertine'. *On the side of the arch is* Clematis 'Alba Luxurians'.

Above: *Clematis tumbling over the corner of a pergola. Here, C. 'Etoile Violette' combines with some late flowers of C.* montana *to create an attractive picture.*

Above: *Colourful foliage makes a long-lasting covering for a pergola. Here* Vitis vinifera *'Purpurea' creates an attractive screen up a wooden pillar. As the year proceeds, the colour of the foliage will deepen, so there is a change of appearance, even without flowers.*

Above: *A romantic walkway created from a series of arches, passing along a clipped path through long grass. The arches provide a delightful tunnel effect, while the statue at the end draws the eye and adds to the romantic image.*

Temporary Supports

It is not always desirable to have fixed screens or supports for climbers. It can be fun to move them around the garden, using a different position each year. This allows a much more flexible design. While this is not really practical with perennial climbers, especially those that might take several years to establish themselves, it is entirely possible with annuals.

USING TEMPORARY SUPPORTS

In some cases, temporary supports can undertake two functions at once: to provide an attractive screen and to provide vegetables for the kitchen. Thus, peas and beans make good traditional subjects, while more novel ideas might include climbing marrows, courgettes (zucchini), gourds (squashes) and cucumbers.

Temporary screens are easy to make and a variety of materials can be used. Many are rustic in nature, such as pea-sticks simply pushed into the ground or traditional bean poles tied together in a row or wigwam (tepee). More modern materials would include plastic netting held on poles or a metal frame. However, it is best not to use materials that are unattractive, as the plants trained up temporary supports do not often get under way until the early summer, not covering them until midsummer.

Temporary structures can also be used for a few perennials that are cut to the ground each year, such as the everlasting pea *Lathyrus latifolius* or some of the clematis that are either herbaceous or a pruned to near the ground each year. Since the latter can grow quite tall, they can be supported by large branches stuck in the ground, to imitate small trees.

Left: *Climbing plants can often be used in this somewhat more horizontal way than is usual. It is an ideal way to utilize space left after spring flowers have finished blooming.*

Above: *A typical bean row, with the scarlet-flowered runner beans climbing up poles that have been tied together for support. The poles can be kept for several seasons before they need to be replaced.*

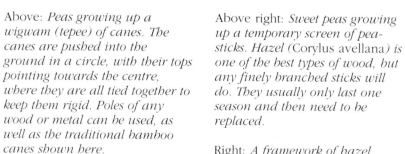

Above: *Peas growing up a wigwam (tepee) of canes. The canes are pushed into the ground in a circle, with their tops pointing towards the centre, where they are all tied together to keep them rigid. Poles of any wood or metal can be used, as well as the traditional bamboo canes shown here.*

Above right: *Sweet peas growing up a temporary screen of pea-sticks. Hazel (Corylus avellana) is one of the best types of wood, but any finely branched sticks will do. They usually only last one season and then need to be replaced.*

Right: *A framework of hazel sticks have been woven into a dome, over which a clematis is growing.*

Growing Climbers in Containers

Although most climbers are grown in the open ground, there is no reason why they should not be grown in containers. This is a particularly good idea for a balcony, roof garden or patio. While it is not really feasible to grow vigorous plants in this way, a surprising number of climbers are suitable.

SUPPORTING CLIMBERS IN POTS

The main problem when growing climbers in pots is finding a method of supporting the plant. If they are only short plants or annuals, such as black-eyed Susan (*Thunbergia*) or nasturtiums, it is perfectly feasible to include the support in the container. You can use canes or a V-shaped piece of trellising, burying the lower end in the pot.

For more vigorous plants, set the containers against a wall on which trellis has been fixed. An alternative is to have strings or tall canes rising from the pot to some suitable fixing on the wall.

One of the main secrets of success with container climbers is to keep them watered well. Feeding also becomes very important, as constant watering leaches out many of the nutrients in the soil.

1 To ensure that the compost in the container is adequately drained it is important to place a layer of small stones or broken pots in the bottom. This will allow any excess water to drain away quickly.

2 Partly fill the pot with a good-quality potting compost (soil mix). Add to this some water-retaining granules and stir these into the compost. Use the quantity recommended on the packet. The granules will expand when they become wet and hold the moisture until the plant wants it, without making the soil too wet, something that most plants hate.

3 Put the narrow end of the trellis into the container. The trellis will be held in position by the weight of the compost, so the base should be as low down in the pot as possible. This type of frame is not suitable for tall, narrow pots, which may be blown over easily.

4 Put the plant in position so that the top of the rootball comes level with the intended surface of the compost. Put in the remaining compost and lightly firm it down. Train the stems of the climber against the trellis and tie them in, if necessary.

5 Water the pot and top it up with compost (soil mix) if the level falls. Cover the top with pebbles or gravel, partly to give it a pleasant appearance but also to help suppress weeds and make watering easier. When creating such a display, put it in its final position before you fill the container as the complete container may be very heavy.

6 As an alternative, fix a piece of trellis to a wall and stand the pot next to it. This will take heavier climbers and be less inclined to blow or fall over. Being next to a wall may put the pot in a rain shadow, however, so be prepared to water it even if you have had rain.

Above: *Grouping containers together presents an attractive display. Here, Clematis 'Prince Charles' is planted in a chimney pot next to some potted chives.*

Above: *A variety of different frameworks can be used in large containers, to support annual and temporary climbers. The metal frameworks will last the longest but will be most expensive. The willow wicker support, at the back of the group, is attractive in its own right.*

Shrubs List

Lists of shrubs for specific purposes (e.g. ground cover) are given in the relevant sections

d = deciduous
e = evergreen

YELLOW-FLOWERED SHRUBS

Azara (e)
Berberis (d & e)
Buddleja globosa (d)
Chimonanthus (d)
Colutea arborescens (d)
Cornus mas (d)
Coronilla (e)
Corylopsis (d)
Corylus (d)
Cytisus (d)
Forsythia (d)
Fremontodendron californicum (e)
Genista (d)
Halimium (e)
Hamamelis (d)
Helianthemum (e)
Hypericum (d)
Jasminum (d & e)
Kerria japonica (d)
Mahonia (e)
Phlomis (e)
Piptanthus (e)
Potentilla (d)
Rhododendron (d & e)
Senecio (d)

Azara lanceolata

ORANGE-FLOWERED SHRUBS

Berberis (d & e)
Buddleja x weyeriana (d)
Colutea orientalis (d)
Embothrium coccineum (e)
Helianthemum (e)
Potentilla (d)
Rhododendron (d & e)

Fuchsia 'Genii'

RED-FLOWERED SHRUBS

Callistemon citrinus (e)
Calluna (e)
Camellia (e)
Chaenomeles (d)
Crinodendron hookerianum (e)

Fremontodendron californicum

Desfontainia spinosa (e)
Erythrina crista-galli (d)
Escallonia (e)
Fuchsia (d)
Helianthemum (e)
Hydrangea (d)
Leptospermum (e)
Rhododendron (d & e)
Ribes speciosum (d)
Weigela (d)

PINK-FLOWERED SHRUBS

Abelia (e)
Andromeda (e)
Buddleja (d)
Calluna (e)
Camellia (e)
Chaenomeles (d)
Cistus (e)

Chaenomeles speciosa 'Moerloosii'

Calluna vulgaris 'Darkness'

Clerodendrum bungei (d)
Cotinus coggygria (d)
Cytisus (d)
Daphne (d & e)
Deutzia (d)
Erica (e)
Escallonia (e)
Fuchsia (d)
Hebe (e)
Helianthemum (e)
Hibiscus (d)
Hydrangea (d)
Indigofera (d)
Kalmia (e)
Kolkwitzia (d)
Lavatera (d)
Leptospermum (e)
Lonicera (d)
Magnolia (d & e)
Nerium (e)
Prunus (d)
Rhododendron (d & e)
Ribes sanguineum (d)
Spiraea (d)
Syringa (d)
Viburnum (d & e)
Weigela (d)

Ceanothus impressus

BLUE-FLOWERED SHRUBS
Buddleja (d)
Caryopteris (d)
Ceanothus (d & e)
Ceratostigma (d)
Hebe (e)
Hibiscus (d)
Hydrangea (d)
Lavandula (e)
Perovskia (d)
Rhododendron (d & e)
Rosmarinus (e)
Vinca (e)

Syringa vulgaris

PURPLE-FLOWERED SHRUBS
Buddleja (d)
Elsholtzia stauntonii (d)
Erica (e)
Hebe (e)
Hydrangea (d)

Rhamnus alaternus 'Variegata'
with *Campanula pyramidalis*

Lavandula stoechas (e)
Rhododendron (d & e)
Salvia officinalis (e)
Syringa (d)
Vinca (e)

WHITE-FLOWERED SHRUBS
Aralia (d)
Berberis thunbergia (d)
Buddleja (d)
Calluna (e)
Camellia (e)
Carpenteria californica (e)
Chaenomeles (d)

Choisya (d)
Cistus (e)
Clerodendrum trichotomum (d)
Clethra alnifolia (d)
Cornus (d)
Cotoneaster (e)
Crataegus (d)
Cytisus (d)
Daphne blagayana (d)
Erica (e)
Escallonia (e)
Eucryphia (d & e)
Exochorda x *macrantha* (d)
Fuchsia (d)
Gaultheria (e)
Halesia (d)
Hebe (e)
Helianthemum (e)
Hibiscus (d)
Hoheria (d)
Hydrangea (d)
Itea (d & e)
Jasminum (d & e)
Leptospermum (e)

Ligustrum (e)
Magnolia (d & e)
Myrtus (e)
Olearia (e)
Osmanthus (e)
Philadelphus (d)
Pieris (e)
Potentilla (d)
Prunus (d)
Pyracantha (e)
Rhododendron (d & e)
Romneya (d)
Rubus 'Tridel' (d)
Sambucus (d)
Skimmia (e)
Spiraea (d)
Stephanandra (d)
Syringa (d)
Viburnum (d & e)
Vinca (e)

GREEN-FLOWERED SHRUBS
Daphne laureola (e)
Garrya elliptica (d)

Carpenteria californica

SHRUBS FOR DRY SHADE
Aucuba japonica (e)
Ilex (d & e)
Pachysandra terminalis (e)
Buxus sempervirens (e)
Daphne laureola (d & e)
Elaeagnus × ebbingei (e)
Gaultheria shallon (e)
Hypericum × inordum 'Elstead' (d)
Lonicera pileata (e)

SHRUBS FOR MOIST SHADE
Camellia (e)
Clethra (d & e)
Corylopsis (d)
Crataegus laevigata (d)
Enkianthus (d)
Fatsia japonica (e)
Fothergilla (d)
Mahonia aquifolium (e)
Osmanthus decorus (e)
Pieris formosa var. *forrestii*
   'Wakehurst' (e)

Rhododendron (d & e)
Salix magnifica (d)
Sarcococca ruscifolia (e)
Skimmia japonica (e)
Viburnum davidii (e)
Vinca major (e)
Vinca minor (e)

SHRUBS FOR SUNNY AND DRY AREAS
Caryopteris × clandonensis (d)
Cistus (e)
Convolvulus cneorum (e)
Cytisus (d & e)
Hamamelis mollis (d)
Helianthemum
   nummularium (e)
Santolina chamaecyparissus (e)
Senecio (e)
Yucca (e)

SHRUBS FOR ACID SOIL
Azalea (d & e)
Calluna vulgaris (e)
Camellia (e)
Corylopsis pauciflora (d)
Daboecia (e)
Enkianthus (d)
Erica cinerea (e)
Fothergilla (d)
Gaultheria mucronata (e)
Halesia carolina (d)
Hamamelis (d)
Kalmia latifolia (e)
Pieris (e)
Rhododendron (d & e)
Ulex europaeus (e)

SHRUBS FOR CHALKY SOIL
Berberis darwinii (e)
Buddleja davidii (d)
Ceanothus impressus (e)
Choisya ternata (e)
Cistus (e)

Clematis (d & e)
Cotoneaster (d & e)
Deutzia (d)
Helianthemum (e)
Lavandula (e)
Nerium oleander (e)
Paeonia suffruticosa (d)
Potentilla (shrubby species) (d)
Pyracantha (e)
Rosa rugosa (shrub species)
Syringa (d)
Viburnum tinus (e)

SHRUBS FOR SANDY SOIL
Calluna vulgaris (e)
Ceanothus thyrsiflorus (e)
Cistus (e)
Cytisus scoparius (d)
Erica arborea alpina (e)
Gaultheria mucronata (e)
Genista tinctoria (d)
Lavandula (e)
Rosa pimpinellifolia (d)

Below: *Rosemary (*Rosmarinus*)
has a distinctive scent.*

Below: *The foliage of* Pieris
japonica *changes through the year.*

Below: Helianthemum *'Wisley
Pink' has unusual silver leaves.*

Rosmarinus officinalis (e)
Spartium junceum (d)
Yucca gloriosa (e)

SHRUBS FOR CLAY SOIL
Clethra alnifolia (d)
Cornus alba 'Sibirica' (d)
Kalmia latifolia (e)
Magnolia (some) (d & e)
Salix caprea (d)
Sambucus racemosa (d)
Viburnum opulus (d)

SHRUBS FOR GROUND COVER
Cotoneaster cochleatus (e)
Erica carnea (e)
Euonymus fortunei (e)
Hypericum calycinum (e)
Juniperus horizontalis (e)
Lonicera pileata (e)
Pachysandra terminalis (e)
Persicaria affinis (e)
Rosa (ground cover species)

Thymus (e)
Vinca minor (e)

SHRUBS THAT ATTRACT WILDLIFE
Buddleja davidii (d)
Cotoneaster species (d & e)
Hebe (e)
Lavandula (e)
Ilex (e)
Pyracantha (e)

SHRUBS WITH FRAGRANT FLOWERS
Buddleja davidii (d)
Chimonanthus praecox (d)
Choisya ternata (e)
Cytisus battandieri (e)
Daphne mezereum (d)
Lavandula (e)
Lonicera fragrantissima (d & e)
Philadelphus (d)
Rosa (d)

Sarcococca (e)
Syringa (d)
Viburnum × *bodnantense* (d)
Viburnum carlesii (d)

SHRUBS WITH SCENTED FOLIAGE
Aloysia triphylla (d)
Artemisia abrotanum (d)
Helichrysum italicum (e)
Hyssopus officinalis (d)
Lavandula (e)
Pelargonium (scented-leaved forms) (e)
Rosmarinus officinalis (e)
Salvia officinalis (e)

SHRUBS FOR HEDGES AND WINDBREAKS
Berberis darwinii (e)
Buxus sempervirens (e)
Cotoneaster simonsii (d)
Elaeagnus × *ebbingei* (e)

Escallonia (e)
Euonymus japonicus (e)
Griselinia littoralis (e)
Lavandula (e)
Ligustrum ovalifolium (e)
Lonicera nitida (e)
Photinia × *fraseri* 'Red Robin' (e)
Pittosporum tenuifolium (e)
Prunus laurocerasus (e)
Prunus lusitanica (e)
Tamarix ramosissima (d)

SHRUBS FOR EXPOSED SITES
Elaeagnus pungens 'Maculata' (e)
Erica cinerea (e)
Euonymus japonicus (e)
Genista hispanica (e)
Hibiscus rosa-sinensis (e)
Hippophäe rhamnoides (d)
Lavandula 'Hidcote' (e)
Pyracantha coccinea (e)
Senecio 'Sunshine' (e)
Viburnum tinus (e)

Below: Choisya ternata *'Sundance'* *has fragrant white flowers.*

Below: Pyracantha *has very decorative autumn berries.*

Below: Salvia officinalis *'Icterina' or sage is often used in cooking.*

Climbers List

Plant lists for specific types of climbers (e.g. fragrant climbers) are given in the relevant sections.

Where only the genus is given several species and cultivars are suitable.

ac = annual climber
c = climber
wf = wall fruit
ws = wall shrub

YELLOW-FLOWERED CLIMBERS AND WALL SHRUBS

Abutilon megapotamicum (ws)
Azara dentata (ws)
Billardiera longiflora (c)
Clematis (c)
  C. 'Moonlight'
  C. 'Paten's Yellow'
  C. rehderiana
  C. tangutica
  C. tibetana

Clematis tangutica

Eccremocarpus scaber (c)
Fremontodendron
  californicum (ws)
Humulus lupulus 'Aureus' (c)
Jasminum (c & ws)
Lathyrus (ac & c)
Lonicera (c)
Magnolia grandiflora (ws)
Piptanthus laburnifolius (ws)
Rosa (c)
  R. 'Dreaming Spires'
  R. 'Emily Grey'
  R. 'Gloire de Dijon'
  R. 'Golden Showers'
Thunbergia alata (ac)
Tropaeolum (ac)

Lonicera japonica *'Halliana'*

ORANGE-FLOWERED CLIMBERS AND WALL SHRUBS

Bignonia capreolata (c)
Bougainvillea spectabilis (c)
Campsis (c)
Eccremocarpus scaber (c)
Lonicera (c)
Rosa (c)
  R. 'Autumn Sunlight'
  R. 'Danse du Feu'
Tropaeolum (ac)

RED-FLOWERED CLIMBERS AND WALL SHRUBS

Akebia quinata (c)
Bougainvillea spectabilis (c)
Callistemon citrinus (ws)
Camellia (ws)
Chaenomeles (ws)

Clematis *'Madame Julia Correvon'*

Clematis *'Comtesse de Bouchard'*

Clematis (c)
  C. 'Niobe'
  C. 'Ruby Glow'
Clianthus puniceus (ws)
Crinodendron hookerianum (ws)
Desfontainea spinosa (ws)
Eccremocarpus scaber (c)
Erythrina crista-galli (ws)
Lathyrus (ac & c)
Lonicera (c)
Phaseolus coccineus (ac)
Rhodochiton atrosanguineum (c)
Ribes speciosum (ws)
Rosa (c)
  R. 'American Pillar'
  R. 'Danny Boy'
  R. 'Excelsa'
  R. 'Galway Bay'
  R. 'Symphathie'
Tropaeolum (ac & c)

Clematis *'Duchess of Albany'*

PINK-FLOWERED CLIMBERS AND WALL SHRUBS

Bougainvillea spectabilis (c)
Camellia (ws)
Chaenomeles (ws)
Cistus (ws)
Clematis (c)
  C. 'Comtesse de Bouchard'
  C. 'Hagley Hybrid'
  C. 'Margot Koster'

Lathyrus grandiflorus

Hoya carnosa (c)
Jasminum beesianum (c)
Jasminum x *stephanense* (c)
Lapageria rosea (c)
Lathyrus (ac & c)
Lonicera (c)
Malus (wf)
Mandevilla splendens (c)

Nerium oleander (ws)
Prunus (wf)
Rosa (c)
    R. 'Albertine'
    R. 'Bantry Bay'
    R. 'New Dawn'
    R. 'Pink Perpétue'
    R. 'Zéphirine Drouhin'

Vinca major

BLUE-FLOWERED CLIMBERS AND WALL SHRUBS

Aloysia triphylla (ws)
Ceanothus (ws)
Clematis (c)
    C. 'Beauty of Richmond'
    C. 'Lady Betty Balfour'
    C. macropetala
    C. 'Mrs Cholmondeley'
    C. 'Perle d'Azur'
Hydrangea aspera villosa (ws)
Ipomoea (ac)
Lathyrus (ac & c)
Passiflora caerulea (c)
Plumbago capensis (c)
Rosmarinus officinalis (ws)
Solanum crispum (ws)
Solanum jasminoides (c)
Sollya fusiformis (c)
Teucrium fruticans (ws)
Vinca major (c)
Wisteria (c)

PURPLE-FLOWERED CLIMBERS AND WALL SHRUBS

Clematis (c)
    C. 'Etoile Violette'

Clematis *'Lasurstern'* and Clematis *'Nelly Moser'*

    C. 'Gipsy Queen'
    C. 'The President'
Cobaea scandens (ac)
Lathyrus (ac & c)
Rosa (c)
    R. 'Bleu Magenta'
    R. 'Veilchenblau'
    R. 'Violette'
Solanum dulcamara 'Variegata' (c)

Vitis vinifera *'Purpurea'*

GREEN-FLOWERED CLIMBERS AND WALL SHRUBS

Garrya elliptica (ws)
Hedera (c)
Itea ilicifolia (ws)
Ribes laurifolium (ws)
Vitis (c)

Clematis *'Mrs George Jackman'*

WHITE-FLOWERED CLIMBERS AND WALL SHRUBS

Camellia (ws)
Carpenteria californica (ws)
Chaenomeles (ws)
Cistus (ws)
Clematis (c)
    C. 'Edith'
    C. 'Miss Bateman'
    C. 'Snow Queen'
Clianthus puniceus (ws)
Cotoneaster (ws)
Dregea sinensis (c)
Fallopia baldschuanica (c)
Hoheria (ws)
Hoya carnosa (c)
Hydrangea anomala petiolare (c)
Jasminum (c & ws)

Clematis florida *'Sieboldii'*

Lathyrus (ac & c)
Mandevilla suaveolens (c)
Myrtus (ws)
Nerium oleander (ws)
Pileostegia viburnoides (c)
Prunus (wf)
Pyracantha (ws)
Pyrus (wf)
Rosa (c)
    R. 'Albéric Barbier'
    R. 'Kiftsgate'
    R. 'Mme Alfred Carrière'
Solanum jasminoides 'Album' (c)
Trachelospermum (c)
Wisteria (c)

Rosa *'Iceberg'* and Clematis tangutica

Clematis *'Marie Boisselot'*

CLIMBERS FOR DRY SHADE
Hedera canariensis (c)
Lapageria rosea (c)
Parthenocissus tricuspidata (c)

CLIMBERS FOR MOIST SHADE
Humulus lupulus 'Aureus'
   (h & c)
Hydrangea petiolaris (c)
Lonicera tragophylla (c)
Pileostegia viburnoides (c)
Schizophragma
   integrifolium (c)

Trachelospermum
   jasminoides (c)

CLIMBERS FOR ACID SOIL
Berberidopsis corallina (c)

CLIMBERS FOR CHALKY SOIL
Campsis radicans (c)
Celastrus orbiculatus (c)
Clematis (all)
Eccremocarpus scaber (c & a)
Hedera (c)
Lonicera (some) (c)

Passiflora caerulea racemosa (c)
Rosa banksiae 'Lutea' (c)
Rosa 'Albertine' (c)
Trachelospermum jasminoides (c)
Wisteria sinensis (c)

CLIMBERS FOR SANDY SOIL
Vitis vinifera 'Purpurea' (c)

CLIMBERS FOR CLAY SOIL
Humulus lupulus 'Aureus' (c)
Rosa filipes 'Kiftsgate' (c)
Vitis coignetiae (c)

CLIMBERS FOR QUICK COVER
Hedera helix (small cvs) (c)
Hydrangea petiolaris (c)
Polygonum
   baldschuanicum (c)
Trachelospermum
   jasminoides (c)

Below: Rosa *'Iceberg' is a beautiful, highly fragrant rose.*

Below: *Hops* (Humulus lupulus) *are good at disguising eyesores.*

Below: Passiflora *is a stunning climber that loves walls.*

CLIMBERS FOR GROUND COVER

Hedera colchica 'Dentata Variegata' (c)

Schizophragma hydrangeoides (c)

Vitis coignetiae (c)

CLIMBERS WITH FRAGRANT FLOWERS

Azara (c)

Clematis montana 'Elizabeth' (c)

Itea ilicifolia (c)
Jasminum (most) (c)
Lathyrus odoratus (c & a)
Lonicera (many) (c)
Osmanthus (c)
Passiflora (c)
Trachelospermum (c)
Wisteria (c)

CLIMBERS WITH ARCHITECTURAL FOLIAGE

Hedera colchica 'Dentata Variegata' (c)

Schizophragma hydrangeoides (c)

Schizophragma integrifolium (c)

Vitis coignetiae (c)

CLIMBERS FOR CONTAINERS

Eccremocarpus scaber (c)
Hedera helix and cvs (c)
Ipomoea (some) (c & a)
Lathyrus (climbing species) (c & a)
Passiflora (c)

CLIMBERS FOR EXPOSED SITES

Euonymus fortunei (c)
Hedera helix (c)
Wisteria sinensis (c)

Below: Campsis radicans *is a beautiful late summer climber.*

Below: Rosa *'Zéphirine Drouhin' is adaptable and has no thorns.*

Below: *The flowers of* Clematis *'Perle d'Azur' open in summer.*

INDEX

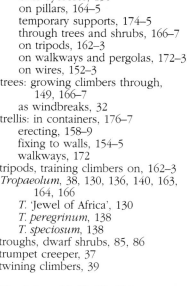

Acknowledgements

The publishers would like to thank the following for their permission to photograph their plants and gardens: Hilary and Richard Bird, Ken Bronwin, Mr and Mrs R Cunningham, Chris and Stuart Fagg, Della and Colin Fox, Christopher Lloyd, Merriments Gardens, Eric Pierson, the RHS Garden Wisley, Mavis and David Seeney, Lyn and Brian Smith.

They would also like to thank the following people for allowing their pictures (to which they own the copyright) to be reproduced in this book:

Key: t = top; b = bottom; r = right; l = left; c = centre

Richard Bird for the picture on p. 61 (br); **Jonathan Buckley** for the pictures on p. 41 (br), p. 81 (br), p. 137 (tr), p. 137 (br), p. 153 (tr), p. 153 (bl), p. 153 (br), p. 162 (tr), p. 170 (b), p. 171 (r), p. 173 (l), p. 174 (br), p. 175 (br), p. 175 (l), p. 176 (all), p. 177 (all); **The Garden Picture Library** for the picture on p. 70; **Andrew Lawson** for the front cover picture; **Peter McHoy** for the pictures on p. 32, p. 33 (br), p. 39 (r), p. 43, p. 52, p. 53, p. 54 (tr), p. 54 (bl), p. 55 (tl), p. 79 (br), p. 97 (tr), p. 102 (tr), p. 103 (tr), p. 110 (tl), p. 110 (tr), p. 112 (br), p. 113 (bl), p. 120 (tr), p. 121 (l), p. 122 (all), p. 123 (tr), p. 123 (br), p. 124 (tl), p. 124 (tr), p. 125 (br), p. 131 (b), p. 135 (bl), p. 138 (br), p. 140 (b), p. 141 (r), p. 142 (br), p. 143 (bl), p. 144 (tr), p. 144 (bl), p. 178 (bl), p. 178 (tc), p. 178 (bc), p. 179 (t), p. 179 (br), p. 182 (c), p. 185 (tl); and **Derek St Romaine** for the picture on p. 69.